£7.50

Dedication

To M.G.U., whose lifelong dedication to Triumph and the Bonneville inspired the completion of this book.

BONNIE

The Development History of the Triumph Bonneville

J. R. Nelson

ISBN 0 85429 257 8

First published 1979
Reprinted 1980, 1981, 1984, 1987, 1989

A FOULIS Motorcycling Book

Published by
Haynes Publishing Group
Sparkford, Nr. Yeovil, Somerset BA22 7JJ, England

Haynes Publications Inc
861 Lawrence Drive, Newbury Park, California 91320 USA

Editor: Rod Grainger
Layout design: Graffiti
Cover design: Phill Jennings
Printed in England by: J.H. Haynes & Co. Ltd.

Preface

It has been claimed that the Triumph Bonneville has become a legend in its own time. Whether or not this is true only time will tell. What is certain is that it has outlasted and survived many of its contemporaries and yet still remains a much sought after 'superbike', both by the young enthusiast of today who may or may not be fully aware of the past glories of the Triumph marque, and also by his forebears who continually seek to restore or refurbish the earlier examples still in service as a practical and pleasant homage to their own enjoyment of yesteryear.

This book is aimed at acquainting the former of the technical progress of the Triumph Bonneville (hereinafter called 'the Bonnie') throughout its long and varied career and also to assist the latter in establishing the technical and design changes that occurred year by year enabling the would-be restorer or enquirer to establish, as far as possible, the correct specification of any Bonnie model ever built.

It should be made clear that the Triumph model T120 Bonneville was not designed from scratch, starting from a completely blank sheet of paper, nor did it 'just happen'. It was the logical outcome of progressive development, stemming from a sound product led by a sure-footed management team, with a positive marketing policy inspiring a unique happy band of enthusiasts within a company that knew exactly where it was going. This team of pioneers was not just randomly assembled from the nearest source of available supply. It was hand picked, moulded and developed by the very small dedicated Board of Directors. The company grew from strength to strength guided by these founding fathers, who continually strove to ensure that what they were attempting to achieve would be the very best for the company itself. From such roots the Bonnie stemmed.

This then is the story of the genealogy and growth of the original and famous Triumph model range culminating in that branch which bore the 650cc model 6T Thunderbird and from which the fruit of their labours, the 'Bonnie', eventually blossomed.

5

Acknowledgements

The author wishes to record his sincere appreciation for the assistance he has received from friends and collegues in the compilation, completion and correction of this book. Principal thanks go to F. S. (Stan) Truslove for the use of his prodigious memory and for his anecdotal re-writing of large sections; to Frank Baker and Henry Vale for Historic material and proof-reading corrections; Harry Woolridge for valuable technical information and assistance in the co-ordination of technical specification and annual model changes, and David Green for much detailed research.

I would also like to acknowledge with thanks the permission given by the Board of Directors of Triumph Motorcycles (Meriden) Ltd. to utilise photographic and technical information still remaining in existence at Meriden, and to Brian Jones for the generous access into the Meriden past-historic specification *sanctum sanctorum*.

And Ivor Davies for yet more photographs.

John Nelson
July 1979

PART ONE

The Bonnie Story

The roots of the family tree

The origin of the Triumph marque goes way back before the turn of the century, for it was in the late 1800s that two young enterprising Germans, one a businessman and the other an engineer, set up business in London selling bicycles. The business, already using the name Triumph, moved to Coventry in 1888 with the intention of manufacturing its own machines. The choice of Triumph as a brand name was simply that it meant the same in most European languages and required little further translation or explanation. The choice of Coventry as a manufacturing location was because the cycle making skills of the city had long been recognised even in those early days of the industry.

Seigfried Bettmann was the businessman and founder of the original company. M. J. Shulte was the engineer who in 1902 was to convert the suitable pedal cycles within the existing range of products to motorised cycles. At first he used the commercially available 'Minerva' and other 'clip-on' engine units of the day, until 1905 when his own 3 horsepower engine was fully developed and fitted. This domestically designed and manufactured unit gained an immediate reputation for reliability and pioneered a remarkable increase in rate of production, development and improvement over the next ten years.

It is interesting to note from the 1914 Triumph Cycle Company Ltd catalogue, which, incidentally, was the first to bear the now well-known Triumph motif, the following extract from an article by W. Whitall originally published in the *OBSERVER*:

'In the years 1903 and 1904, it looked as though the motorcycle had taken a permanent hold on the younger generation and those who used the roads, and that nothing remained to do but to develop the machine and build up a sound and permanent industry. But in those days the machine itself was unreliable to a degree, and in spite of all the efforts that were made to improve the dependability, it really began to look as though the task were hopeless.

And at last, motorcycles almost ceased to be made in the factories of Coventry.

Siegfried Bettman, the founder of the original Triumph Cycle Company in London in 1885, moving to Much Park Street in Coventry in 1888, and becoming Mayor of the City in 1913-14, and President of the British Cycle and Motorcycle Manufacturers Association from 1928 - 1929

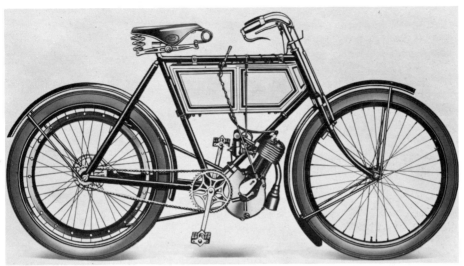

The 1902 Model Triumph, using a Belgian Minerva side valve engine. The drive was direct, via a belt, to the rear wheel, without either clutch or gearbox

There was one firm, however, which never wavered in its opinion that one day all the difficulties would be overcome, and motorcycling would come into its legitimate own. That firm was the Triumph cycle company, to whom credit is due for its unwavering faith in the possibilities of the future. The influence for good which the Triumph company has exercised on motorcycling is almost incalculable.'

These words, written over sixty years ago, still have the same ring of truth and apply equally today. They could not have been earned other than by dedication and application of continual and realistic development and distribution of a product appropriate and attractive

1911 Triumph TT 3½ HP Tourist Trophy Racer. 85 x 88mm side valve with Triumph registered design variable pulley, Triumph carburetter, magneto ignition, 26 x 2¼ in. wheels and 1¼ gal. fuel tank

to the market place of the day.

It is also interesting to note that according to that same catalogue, the 4 horsepower model had been added to the range, and the three-speed version could be purchased for £60 cash or £65 on instalment or exchange terms. A Tourist Trophy Racer version was offered at £56, with the then cheapest 3½ horsepower version at £49 15s 0d.

The 1915 catalogue prefaced its first page with 'contractors to the British, French, Belgian and Russian War Offices' and introduced a 2¼ horsepower Junior Triumph at £42. All quoted horsepower at that time were RAC ratings calculated on the basis that one RAC horsepower was equal to 100 cubic centimetres of cylinder capacity.

The Model 'H' was first featured in that same catalogue, with its chain-cum-belt drive as it was then called. In its World War I 'call-up' guise it soon became known as the despatch rider's 'Trusty Triumph' and a quantity of something like 30,000 were produced and issued. Again, a quote from the 1915 catalogue was from an Army despatch rider 'who did not wish to have his name disclosed' extolling the virtue and reliability of his machine in military service 'over paved roads, deep mud, ditches, gates, raised railway lines and indescribable roads'.

After the war, motorcycling literature indicated that many thousands of ex-soldiers, having been pressed into military despatch riding service, had come to rely on and trust their Triumph model 'H' so much that with the end of the hostilities a new generation of motorcycle enthusiasts had evolved. The widespread knowledge that the Triumph had proved to be so reliable in times of need provided the factory in Coventry with an immediate demand and an ever increasing market for its products.

By 1927, for instance, the production rate had topped 30,000 machines per year. Mass production methods had reduced prices to £39 10s 0d for the 2 horsepower model with Lucas acetylene lamps and bulb horn, or £43 15s 0d with Lucas Magdyno electric lamps up

Imagine the sheer luxury of the coachbuilt Gloria sidecar Model B, finished in Parma Violet, and with upholstery in grey antique Pegamoid cloth. It was claimed that the "Cee springs at the front and the half elliptic springs at the rear – effectively eliminate all shocks and bounce" – all for eighteen guineas!

to an expensive £62 15s 0d for the big 5½ horsepower SD model. Incidentally, the Triumph Gloria sidecars were now available at £11 17s 6d complete with chassis frame, all attachments, wheel and Dunlop cord tyre with a really de luxe version at £18 18s 0d! The name 'Gloria', commemorating the famous beauty of the day, was later to be used again when Triumph became involved in car production.

It was shortly after the end of the First World War that M. J. Shulte retired and Lieutenant Colonel Holbrook was appointed Managing Director. This appointment coincided with an immediate end to any further participation in TT racing activities. This decision, although short lived, proved to be quite a sensation in the press of the day. It is not known to what manner of lobbying was due the return to competitive activities but we do know that the Triumph company were soon to be chasing records and achieving racing successes and TT victories once more.

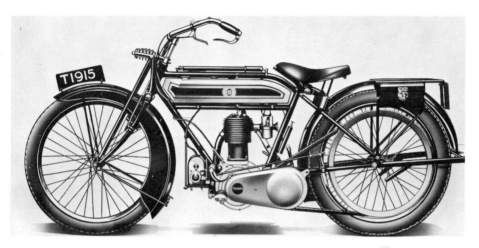

The 1915 Model H 4 HP Triumph Roadster, with Sturmey-Archer three speed countershaft gearbox. The catalogue of the day stated clearly that "the new engine gives greater power than those of previous years, while the easy starting is a special feature due to the improved decompressor

A study of the results from the very early days of the Isle of Man TT races, where stamina, grit and determination, a sound practical knowledge and the carrying of a spare tyre and tube (in addition to drive belt and various other components) were an absolute necessity, will indicate many Triumph successes.

By the year 1922, Henry Ricardo (later to become Sir Henry) had designed and developed a 3½ horsepower engine which had a 'penthouse roof' cylinder head containing four pushrod operated valves. Five years later, this was offered as a TT model having been further developed into a 4.98 horsepower machine. It specified all-chain drive (primary and secondary), engine shaft shock absorber, multi-plate clutch enclosed in an oil bath transmission case, drum brakes front and rear, 'Brooklands' type silencer and a hand change, three speed gearbox. It also boasted that 'the kick-start is totally enclosed, with a special backfire safety mechanism'. Obviously, product liability risks had not raised their ugly head in those days, as a present day publicity man would be prevented by his legal advisers from committing his company to such a claim!

By 1930 the roots of the Triumph Company had been well and truly set and, with reliability as the keynote, had taken well. From the literature of the period, and listening to the surviving members of the 'old firm' it is evident that the company's internal affairs and policies changed. This led to concentration on the development of four-wheeled 13

The 4 valve "Penthouse – Roof" cylinder head "Riccy" 3½ HP OHV Triumph fast Roadster Type R, equipped ready for the road with magdyno lighting set and bulb horn. The catalogue for 1923 also pointed out that features of this machine, were great departures from conventional design. The chief distinguishing feature being that of the engine, incorporating several important patents. It had been designed "in conjunction with Mr. Ricardo, the well-known engineer

John Y. Sangster, founder of the Triumph Engineering Company Limited in 1936, photographed on the occasion of his farewell dinner to his long serving colleagues on the 6th February 1970. Also in the photograph are (left) Ivor Davies, Publicity Manager and (Centre) Jack Wickes, Chief Stylist and Project Engineer

transportation. However, like most other companies in the 30s, the economic depression that existed had a disastrous effect on both them and their customers. It was said that although Triumph works entry cars won the famous Le Mans 24-hour race three years in succession and so made a hat-trick of it, the financial burden of such projects at that time led to the eventual bankruptcy and closure of the Triumph Company, and the end of both car and motorcycle production.

In fact, it was in 1936 that the end finally came. The residue was thus disposed of with the result that the pedal cycle interest was taken over by the Raleigh Cycle Company of Nottingham, the car business by the Standard Motor Company of Coventry, and the ruins of the motorcycle side of the business taken over by John Y. Sangster, son of the Sangster family who had nurtured the Ariel car and motorcycle company in nearby Birmingham through thick and thin. It became a well-known fact that to enable him to execute this 'rescue', John Sangster invested everything he had and more.

It is interesting to note here that the all-familiar Triumph logo with the tail of the letter 'R' extending beneath the remainder of the word sweeping up to link the cross bar of the final letter 'H', with the whole word surmounting a facsimile of the world (as used on very early Triumph motorcycles) may still be seen today on the headstock of currently manufactured cycles, and was in fact used on Triumph cars until quite recently.

THE GROWTH

So it was that the Triumph Engineering Company was first formed. John Sangster immediately acquired the services of Managing Director and Chief Designer in Edward Turner who had already exhibited considerable success and competence at the Ariel Company, with his involvement with their then current range of models, especially the famous 'Square-Four' model. One wonders if it were ever envisaged in those early days that Edward was to become the colossus of the British motorcycle industry that the years ahead were to prove.

Nevertheless these two men proceeded to set their seal upon the company's activities and attitude to such an extent that forty years later the product still contained the essence of the spirit and traditions set at that time.

The range of models existing at the time of collapse of the old Triumph company had already been subjected to a re-design operation by Turner's predecessor, Chief Designer Val Page, and Edward was soon to apply his undoubted genius for sensing the practical, producible, and above all profitable, potential. From this genius came the new range of single cylinder machines, the sports versions to be designated Tiger models, and a twin cylinder engine.

Edward Turner, Managing Director and Chief Designer of the newly formed Triumph Engineering Company in 1936. He is remembered principally for the introduction and impact of the Triumph Speed Twin and Tiger models on the motorcycling world of the day, although his genius and outstanding design ability carried forward the Company successfully for over twenty five years.

The 1938 Speed Twin. The 500cc OHV Twin cylinder Triumph Speed Twin model in Amaranth Red, with Lucas magdyno, and chromed petrol tank, incorporating an instrument panel complete with remote inspection light, with Amaranth Red side panels, lined gold. Frame, guards, oil tank and tool box were all finished in the attractive Amaranth Red paint

1939 Pre-war 500cc OHV twin cylinder Tiger 100 model in chrome and silver (lined black). A most attractive and advanced machine for its day and tremendously popular with the sports rider of the period. The '100' indicated the 100 mph potential which few would not achieve when capably ridden

Inspired by Val's 1934 633cc version, the Turner model was more compact, lighter and had a combined cylinder capacity of 500 cubic centimetres. This then was the birth of the legendary 500cc model Speed Twin to be followed in 1938 by a more sporty version, the model T100 christened, naturally, the Tiger 100. No other engine format had ever made such impact on the industry and it was destined to become the subject of many years of copying by other manufacturers, but none were quite so light, fleet of foot or as thoroughly reliable as the original 5T/T100 Triumph twins.

The intervention of World War II in 1939 was responsible for the company becoming involved in other activities in addition to making military motorcycles. Perhaps the most odd ball was the design and development of a one-man tank project, powered of course by a motorcycle engine. It proved to be rather less than successful and turned out to be far more dangerous for the driver than it could ever possibly have been to an enemy! There was, however, the twin cylinder engine hydraulic service trolley used in aircraft ground servicing, and a similarly powered 24 volt electrical device used by RAF maintenance crews together with a portable airborne electric generator known as the AAPP, (or A-squared, P-squared, as it was known in the experimental department).

The Bomb. Clearance and salvage work came to an abrupt halt when the discovery was made. The filler cap retaining the explosive within this particular missile was eventually chrome plated and used as an ash tray for many years at Meriden in the senior staff dining room

However, on the night of November 14th/15th 1940 the *Luftwaffe* put a stop to all activites when the city of Coventry was blitzed and the city centre where the factory was situated was almost wiped out. The works received its share of direct hits and was to all intents completely destroyed. Typical of the times, the management and workers started to salvage from the rubble any usable tools, office equipment, remnants of machines and machinery immediately it was thought safe to do so. Needless to say, this salvage operation came to rather an abrupt halt when a large unexploded bomb was discovered amongst the debris! A further operation stopped by the holocaust was the future development of a lightweight 350cc twin cylinder machine designated the 3TW, intended for military service. Its ultimate derivative did eventually emerge after the war, very 'civilianised', as the model 3T.

But to return to the story. All the salvaged material was transported to a disused building located on the canal side at Warwick and production, mostly of replacement parts, recommenced. Many tales were told about long serving members leaving the new works, tired and weary from many hours of overtime, who had spent years turning left at the gates of the Coventry factory to journey home, doing so at Warwick instead of turning right and, in wartime blackout, walking straight into the canal!

These days of maximum effort are still remembered with affection by the stalwarts of the older generation but it was not long before the 'shadow factory' in the newly declared 'green-belt' between Coventry and Birmingham at Meriden was completed in order to continue with the war effort. The majority of the motorcycles produced in the new factory were the ohv and side valve versions of the 350cc single cylinder models. The side valve model was built almost to pre-war specification (except for the khaki paint) and was known as the 3SW. The ohv version differed from its pre-war brother by not having separate aluminium rocker boxes but, in view of the wartime shortage of aluminium, a new cylinder head had been designed in which the rocker boxes were integrally cast into the cast iron material. This machine was known as the 3HW model.

The 350cc OHV 3TW Model in its war-time khaki finish and full Military specification, production of which was totally halted by the bombing of Coventry in November 1940. This particular version incorporated a generator within the primary chaincase, whereas the actual military contract machines had a direct lighting generator incorporated in the timing cover. Parking lights were via ordinary torch dry cell batteries housed in a small container under the saddle

Following the end of the Second World War, the Speed Twin and Tiger 100 models re-emerged in their pre-war livery of Amaranth Red for the Speed Twin and Silver Sheen for the Tiger 100, with the return of the now usual chrome-plated parts. A decision had been taken to cease production of the single cylinder models but there was now an addition to the range. It was the civilian successor to the earlier wartime developed 350cc twin, designated the 3T de luxe, looking extremely smart in black and chrome with white lining. Although it was intended to produce a sports version of the 3T; to be known as the Tiger 85, owing to production capacity problems caused by the continually increasing demand for the larger 500cc models, this was not to be.

All these post-war machines were fitted with telescopic front forks, had separate magneto and dynamo (in comparison with the pre-war MagDyno) and the speedometers were now driven from the rear wheel. Once again, Triumph were ready to compete for the world markets.

In competition, the Tiger 100 was soon to show its paces by winning the 1946 Manx Grand Prix. This machine was fitted with an aluminium alloy cylinder head and cylinder block taken from a wartime generator and was to be the fore runner of the Grand Prix racing

The immediately post-war civilianised version of the 3HW 350cc single overhead valve model, finished in black, with white lining and the absolute minimum of chromium plate

The 1951 model 350cc OHV twin 3T De-Luxe. The petrol tank this year reverted to a black paint finish, with aluminium side panel styling strips in response to a world-wide shortage of chromium at the time. Although bearing a family resemblance to the wartime 3TW model, there were very few of the original parts that remained common with this later machine

model, of which 175 were produced. Each of these machines was to go to a private owner as no works riders were ever employed in Edward Turner's day, although some selected riders enjoyed a certain amount of 'back door' assistance. It is doubtful if Edward was aware of this (or was he?)

The ill-fated Tiger 85. This attractive 350cc machine was intended to be a sports version of the 3T twin, but production problems caused by the demand for 500cc models, prevented its manufacture

The successes achieved by the Tiger 100 in the Clubman races, and the Grand Prix models in the 'proper' races of the day, could well have turned the head of many a Managing Director of a motorcycle company towards increasing his involvement in the glamorous racing world, but not Edward Turner. He had a positive fixation that any involvement in racing activities other than producing (and selling) the machines would lead the company straight into bankruptcy. His policy regarding normal production models was very clear indeed. It was to achieve a standard of reliability that would ensure that each and every one of the Triumph products would complete at least 20,000 miles without any undue mechanical attention 'straight off the production line, my boy'. This was a feat that not many of the then opposition was capable of claiming, and to this end the whole company was dedicated.

There were always odd exceptions to the rules, however, and the bark of 'straight-throughs' or the bellow of megaphoned exhausts could often be heard across the fields at Meriden emanating from 'secret' engines running on the test beds within the factory. At these times it could invariably be guaranteed that Edward would be away in Los Angeles, Baltimore or at least in London, on some business trip. Nevertheless some of the rebels were occasionally caught red-handed, busily engaged on the dynamometers in the test shop, doing what came naturally.

The Triumph Grand Prix racer – This photograph shows Ernie Lyons' 1946 M.G.P. winning model

The Triumph T100 Grand Prix engine unit. Illustrating clearly its wartime stationary generator engine origins, with forward parallel exhaust port adaptors and cylinder fin cast bosses originally incorporated as attachment points for the air cooling cowling and ducting

Typical of the Tiger 100 machines being prepared at the factory ("it's-ours!") for racing events at the time. This particular machine was ridden by Maurice Lowe of New Zealand in the 1955 Senior TT and was in the running for the Commonwealth Cup (Lapping at 88mph) Edward Turner was actually seen smiling until a piston failed due to a blocked main jet. The chief conspirator Frank Baker was consigned to Saudi Arabi for a cooling-off period as a result!

The words, 'It's ours!' will always bring a wry smile to the faces of some of those who worked at Meriden in those days. It was the reply to Edward Turner's question, 'That looks nice, whose is it?'. This was asked of one well-known character found lovingly attending a rather special Tiger 100 prior to its being presented to the 'weigh-in' the day before a Senior TT back in the 50s. Edward had arrived in the Isle of Man some 24 hours before he was expected! (Did he know something?). Such efforts, (and well he knew it) kept his, and the company's nose ahead of all but the most serious competition of the day and led to what has now become the lucrative business of producing and marketing 'racing goodies'.

Such components were never fitted as original equipment to any machine on the production line. Edward Turner's philosophy was simply that if anyone owning a Triumph felt he was capable of successfully riding in races, and using every bit of available performance from his machine, then lo! for a bit of extra money he was able to procure a kit for a selection of High Performance parts (please note, never racing parts), fit them himself (thereby absolving everyone else) and discover just how good he was. Edward's often declared philosophy then extended to a continually quoted phrase – and if he then finds he's any good at all, he can start saving up to buy himself a Manx Norton!

This then, was the attitude adopted by Edward Turner (therefore, the company) towards the road racing scene. On the other side of the competition coin, scrambling and trials, where one of the prime objectives was machine reliability (that word again), the attitude was quite different. A Competition Department had been established at Meriden almost immediately after the end of the war and the first machines to be prepared for battle were based on the new 350cc twin. In the hands of that great all-rounder Allan Jefferies, in company with his team partner Jimmy Alves, these machines were soon to make their mark. Countless local and national trials were won whilst development proceeded, culminating in the 500cc TR5 Trophy model which, like the earliest Grand Prix road racer, utilised the wartime AAPP alloy head and cylinder block.

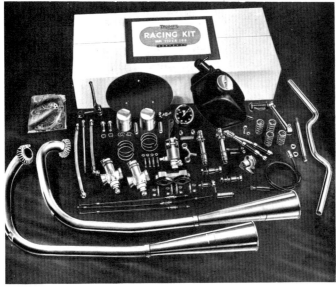

Comprises the following :—

(1) PISTONS. Complete with rings. Choice of Compression Ratios—see page 28.

(2) CAMSHAFTS. Two, racing lift type.

(3) VALVE SPRINGS. Four pairs racing type, inner and outer.

(4) CARBURETTERS. Two Amal Type 6 complete with special dual manifold and 'remote' float chamber.

(5) Dual THROTTLE CABLES with junction box.

(6) PETROL PIPES. Two racing type, flexible.

(7) TACHOMETER. Smiths 8000 R.P.M. with cable drive and gearbox.

(8) OIL TANK one gallon capacity with quick release filler cap.

(9) EXHAUST PIPES. Two small diameter with megaphones.

(10) FOOTREST. One folding pattern.

(11) HANDLEBAR. Racing type.

(12) NUMBER PLATE. One regulation oval pattern with brackets.

(13) BRAKE ROD. One short rear.

(14) KICKSTARTER with folding pedal.

(15) JOINTING WASHERS AND GASKETS. One complete set.

Note. All the above parts are available separately, if required, from the Service Department at usual list prices. Also available are Close Ratio Gears and Racing type alloy Mudguards.

Illustrations of the T100 Racing Kit, from the original Triumph booklet "Tuning the Triumph T100." (c. 1950)

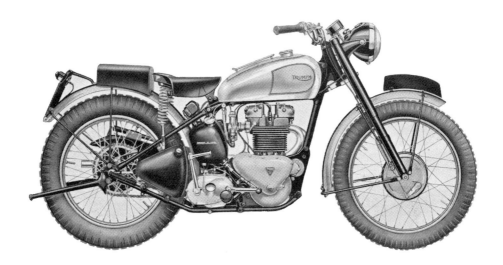

The 1950 Triumph 500cc TR5 Trophy trials machine. Light in weight, outstandingly easy to handle and with an engine specification particularly suitable for reliable slow traction, with ample power for high speeds when necessary, and illustrating well the further utilisation of the war-time generator engine unit

Triumph rear sprung wheel hub. The central square sectioned spring box was curved to allow the wheel to follow the radius from the gearbox drive sprocket to ensure a constant drive chain tension. The 2¼ inches of movement proved to be ideal for the sidecarist. This illustration shows the Mk.2 version

So that was the thinking in the early 50s. Reliability was still the watchword during all the development work. It was also at this time that rear suspension was considered to be an absolute must. Edward Turner, as always wary of any drastic changes in design (unless absolutely essential), introduced the revolutionary Spring Wheel which was designed to fit into the existing frame. In 1947 this was offered as an optional extra at £20 and slipped directly into production causing no hold-up whatever to the flow of machines leaving the line.

Although the incorporation of rear suspension, the tidying up of the headlamp area by setting the lamp in a combined nacelle and instrument panel in 1949, together with a tank top parcel grid and various other quiet modifications kept the models ahead of the opposition, the fast expansion of the all-important American market, where, traditionally, big motorcycles had always ruled the roost, indicated that additional performance would greatly assist sales. By 1950, this theme was heavily endorsed by the directors of the American distribution centres when, on their visits to Meriden, they talked incessantly of the importance of winning local and national competition events, and pulled out all the stops in attempting to persuade their English masters to agree to the New World's theory that 'when it comes to performance, there is no substitute for cubic inches'.

Triumph distribution from the East Coast of America was handled by the Triumph Corporation Incorporated, situated at Towson near Baltimore, Maryland, founded and painstakingly run by Denis McCormack an expatriate Englishman with engineering in his genes (he was actually born in Coventry). He was more than ably assisted on the service side by Rod Coates, Service Manager, who had won the famous Daytona race in 1946 on a Triumph Tiger 100, when part of the course was on the actual beach itself. Their constant

The Triumph headlight and instrument nacelle, typical of the forward design conception of the Edward Turner era

efforts to keep their dealer network fully trained and technically informed of all possible service commitments, coupled with a healthy flow of racing assistance and technical advice based on their own development efforts and aimed at increasing performance, resulted in Coast to Coast successes in the competition field, which proved to be the spur to both the factory in England and, of course, the opposition.

Their prime rivals, in very healthy competition, were the Triumph West Coast distributors, Johnson Motors Incorporated, originally formed prior to the Second World War, and headed by 'Big Bill' Johnson at Pasadena in California. E. W. (Pete) Colman was billed as Parts Manager. Pete had considerable pre-war experience of success in dirt track events from London to Australia, and the parts manager's job was only part of his activity. Pete was also the West Coast motorcycle tuner *par excellence* and constantly sought to keep his expertise and projects ahead of the rest of the field.

However, the time was soon to come when it was realised on both sides of the Atlantic that to continue to satisfy the demand for extra performance something more than high compression ratios, larger diameter valves and ever more ferocious camshaft profiles, was needed. It was then that Edward Turner, perhaps concerned with the risk to the coveted reliability reputation of his products that the efforts of over-enthusiastic tuners might create, finally succumbed to the request to 'substitute any further trend in this direction with the more logical and important cubic inches.'

THE BRANCH

The cylinder capacity chosen was 650cc, of which some experience already existed, albeit via Val Page's 1934 engine. The resultant complete machine was to be made as the 6T Thunderbird. Whilst it could be said the 6T engine was a beefed-up Speed Twin, it certainly was not a hotted-up Speed Twin. It could punch its way across Europe or the USA on post-war low octane fuels at 90 mph plus, almost all day, and yet was as versatile and attractive as the Speed Twin itself about town. To prove the powers the Thunderbird could command Edward decided to put on a bit of a show.

So it was on a cold day (20th September 1949) that a team of riders comprising Allan Jefferies, Jimmy Alves, Bob Manns, Alex Scobie and Len Bayliss and a back-up team led by H. G. Tyrell-Smith, Experimental Chief, and the foreman of the department Ernie Nott, both road racing stars of the 30s, descended on the race track at Montlhéry, near Paris. Having ridden three bikes all the way there, the team then proceeded to cover 500 miles side by side averaging over 90 miles an hour, with a final lap of honour at over 100 mph.

By this no mean feat the arrival of the Big Chief Thunderbird was announced to the motorcycling world. Although today such an effort would probably be called a promotional gimmick, it must be remembered that nothing like it had ever been previously achieved nor was to be repeated for many a long day to come. Nevertheless, here was the precursor of the subject of our story – 'The Bonnie'.

The success of the Montlhéry exercise was acclaimed and welcomed by the journalists and technical press of the time and featured greatly at the Earls Court show that year. Of course, no one ever breathed a word about the Thunderbird that had carried the rotund and

Monthlery, 20th September 1949. Edward Turner with *(Left to Right)* Alex Scobie, Len Bayliss and Bob Manns. The first three 650cc Thunderbird production machines covered 500 miles each at an average of over 90 miles per hour, finishing with a final triumphant lap, ridden side-by-side at over 100 mph, a feat not previously achieved by any other manufacturer

weighty Ernie Nott back to the factory after the venture (yes, they rode them back as well!). Its engine had been slightly seized at Dunstable when Ernie, leading the field as he often did in his pre-war racing days, held on to a wide open throttle just a little too long whilst fighting a very strong headwind. Anyway, there was no need for the engine to be run at the show, so no one would hear the resultant rattle. Perhaps it did indicate that a trifle more development work would be needed before the production of the model commenced for real!

As many older readers will remember, the Thunderbird became the sidecar rider's dream machine. 'Chairs' were still very popular at the time and a 6T with its sweet and flexible engine could haul the current double adult sidecar anywhere one wished to go, with none of the vices of a big thumping single cylinder machine which had previously been necessary for this mode of transport.

With the advent of the 650cc engine, the 500cc range was not to be ignored by the company. In 1948 a very successful factory variant of the 500cc Tiger 100 competition model became available to the general public as the TR5 Trophy model, inevitably resulting in the older 350cc 3T de luxe disappearing the following year in the wake of production rationalisation, now that 'big brother' Thunderbird was with us. This new Trophy model, its engine based on the alloy Tiger 100 unit was, it was claimed, a tough light machine for 'off the road' riders. The name Trophy was to commemorate Triumph winning four International Six Day Trials team awards in 1948, '49, '50 and '51. The first Trophys were built by Henry Vale in the Competition Department in 1947/8, whereas the 1947 ISDT teams were in fact equipped with Speed Twin engine bottom halves and alloy generator set top ends fitted into highly modified lightweight frames.

In 1952, an engine driveshaft alternator system of electrical current generation was fitted to the standard production 5T Speed Twin. This necessitated the abandonment of the long established engine driveshaft shock absorber and resulted in a clutch shaft shock absorber which, with the alternator, still features on models 25 years later.

As one can imagine the Thunderbird was more than welcome in America. It was eagerly siezed upon by the local tuning wizards who found to their delight that it really responded to the same sort of treatment they had meted out to the earlier 500cc models. Their higher octane fuels meant higher compression ratios. Cylinder heads were re-ported and gas flowed, cams with alarming profiles found their way into crankcases as did roller cam followers and a new series of world competition successes were soon achieved. The results of these 'amateur' efforts were filtered back to the factory, with more than a little assistance from Denis McCormack, Rod Coates and Pete Colman, and it would appear that someone was taking notice this time for in 1954, the year incidentally that the lightweight 150cc Terrier was introduced, the Tiger version of the Thunderbird came onto the scene.

This model had a new swinging fork rear suspension, higher compression ratio, bigger valves and ports and, under a very innocent part number E3325, the much sought after 'Q' sports camshaft. As Q1481/2 it was previously obtainable only to those who had access to the Corridors of (B.H.) Power.

What a beautiful, tractable machine it was. Aptly named the T110 model Tiger 110, its searing acceleration was second to none in its class. Two consecutive road test reports in the motorcycling press gave a consistent top speed of 117 miles per hour which, from a machine fitted only with a single carburetter and in full touring trim, was a fair basis for further development and had the feel of a production road racer about it.

By 1955 a further addition to the range appeared in the form of the Tiger Cub. This was a 200cc version of the 150cc Terrier and was to prove to be so much in demand that it eventually ousted the Terrier from the scene altogether. However, 1956 was to be the year of real achievement as far as the 650cc Triumph was concerned. On September 6th, diminutive Johnny Allen, who hailed from Fort Worth, Texas rode (or drove) a fully streamlined projectile across the famous Salt Flats at Bonneville, Utah, at a speed of 214 miles per hour,

The model depicted is the 1957 version of the very successful 650cc Tiger 110, with alloy cylinder head and two-tone (Ivory/Blue) optional extra finish

Wellesbourne Aerodrome, 6th November 1956. Johnny Allan prepares to board the streamliner prior to a demonstration run before BBC television cameras

thereby claiming the World Motorcycle Speed Record. The machine was powered by an unsupercharged Thunderbird engine, running on nitro-methane fuel. The engine was built from standard Triumph parts as were the gearbox, transmission and wheels. As the 1957 catalogue described, it was 'a striking testimony to their design'.

Of all the many glittering successes achieved up to that time by Triumph products in the hands of earnest enthusiasts throughout the world, this one had a place of pride in the hearts of the Men of Meriden that no one could ever take away. The entire project had been initiated and pursued to success by one of the first Triumph dealers to become established in the USA., Pete Dalio (or Big Dee as he was affectionately known), with J. H. (Stormy) Mangham, an American Airlines pilot and motorcycle racer who designed the streamliner and Jack Wilson, the tuning inspiration of the team.

After the success at Bonneville the bike was shipped, by air, to Meriden. No similar operation had ever previously been carried out during the life of the company ('just think of the expense involved!'). In those days any such action was calculated out against the number of machines that would have to be sold to pay for it. 'Is it worth it?' had a truly poignant meaning in a company controlled by Edward Turner and Company Secretary, C. W. F. Parker, or 'Bud' as he was affectionately known (but *not* in his presence!), where one had to produce a pencil used to the last inch before a new one could be requisitioned.

Anyway, the interest and excitement caused by the machine's presence at Meriden is not hard to imagine. Also showing interest was BBC Television who expressed a desire to feature it and the great Johnny Allen on their weekly *Sports View* programme, if only they could film it in action. The prospect of millions of viewers seeing this remarkable machine was understandably immediately siezed upon by the sales and publicity departments who, without any hesitation, arranged for the demonstration runs to take place on the airfield at Wellesbourne, near Warwick.

However, on the day before the runs were scheduled it was discovered that the fuel tank, unseen when the bodywork was in place, had been removed in Texas, prior to the machine being loaded on the plane, and Jack Wilson had removed the pushrods from the engine ('to give the valve springs a well earned rest') after the record had been broken. The kick-start pedal, with its extended shaft which passed through the bodywork to mate up with a 'dog' drive machined on the end of the original kickstart shaft in the gear box, had also been 'left at home'.

Nevertheless the runs took place as arranged, thanks to two Meriden mechanics who worked until well after midnight fabricating a kick-start and a fuel tank from a pre-1954 Speed Twin tool box, making up fuel pipes after finding a suitable place beneath the streamlined shell to hang the fuel tank, and fitting the pushrods after having changed the pistons to allow the engine to be safely run on standard pump petrol. Owing to the late hour, and with due respect to the Meriden neighbourhood, (although it *was* Bonfire Night) it was decided to delay any attempt to start the engine until the following morning. Due to the limited time available on the following day the bodywork was refitted, which meant that if the engine was to need any further attention to enable it to be started, a very quick removal of the bodywork would have to be made. One can imagine the look of relief on the tired faces of the two mechanics at 8 am the following morning of the 6th November 1956 when, in true Triumph fashion, the engine started first kick.

With the 'demo' runs completed and the results of the *Sports View* cameramen's efforts 'in the can', the machine was returned to the factory for clean-up and transportation to BBC's Lime Grove Studios for the live show in company with Johnny Allen who was interviewed by the then head of BBC TV Sport, Peter Dimmock. From there the machine was taken to Earls Court to be proudly displayed standing on a layer of genuine Bonneville salt, atop a giant plinth. It was only on the second day of the show that all the Triumph staff in attendance realised that their perpetual thirst and cracked lips were not due to the customary continual customer chat, but were the effects of that damned imported salt!

Naturally, after the record breaking events, the demand for a Triumph with higher performance than that given by the production T110 model increased, but the policy of the company in this matter remained steadfast. 'If you really wish to take your machine onto the

Keep it upright! *(Left to Right)* – Jim Cooper, Frank Baker, Stan Truslove, and Johnny Allan – almost seated comfortably – A. N. Other, Vic Willoughby and Jack Wilson (Tuner)

"Cameras rolling". The very high speed Triumph 'Thunderbird' on the move.... In an English setting

Motorcycle Show, Earls Court, London, 1956. In recognition of his record-breaking run, Johnny Allen is presented with a water colour painting. (*Left to Right*) Edward Turner, Robert B. Parke (1st Secretary US Embassy), Ivor Davies, Johnny Allen, Jack Wilson (Allen's engine tuner)

race track, we will manufacture a limited number of High Performance components (again this non-racing terminology) which we will allow (note that also) you to purchase for money!'

So it was that camshaft, pistons, valves, valve springs, exhaust pipes, megaphones and other 'hot' bits became available and reports of increased competition successes appeared in the motorcycling press.

At this time, fuels of higher octane rating became readily available which allowed higher than the then standard compression ratios to be used. To combat the increased combustion temperatures that the non-standard ratios generated, a brand new cylinder head die had been laid down in 1955 to produce a light alloy cylinder head which, because of its shape, was known at Meriden as the Delta head. This was fitted to the T110 and new TR6 models in 1956 and had been designed to allow the external rocker box drainpipes to be eliminated, the oil draining direct from the head down through the pushrod cover tubes. The new TR6 was given the name Trophy as had the earlier TR5 500cc model. This meant that three 650cc Triumphs, known in America as the Forty Cubic Inch range, were now available and it was thought that this would suit all tastes. The TR6 was equipped with a chrome-plated headlamp instead of the now traditional nacelle and could be obtained with either Trials or Trials Universal tyres and was an immediate success as a competition machine as well as a high speed road tourer. It scored a legion of successes from gold medals in the International Six Days Trial year after year to many firsts, seconds and thirds in Catalina and Big Bear runs in the United States. Nevertheless, the seemingly insatiable Americans continued to press the factory for even more performance.

In 1957, the 500cc Tiger 100 was offered with a twin carburetter splayed inlet port cylinder head, made from the 650cc Delta casting. This created an almost uncontrollable demand for a similar ported 650cc version from both American Coasts, especially from Rod Coates and Pete Colman who had been spending many hours welding up and boring out the

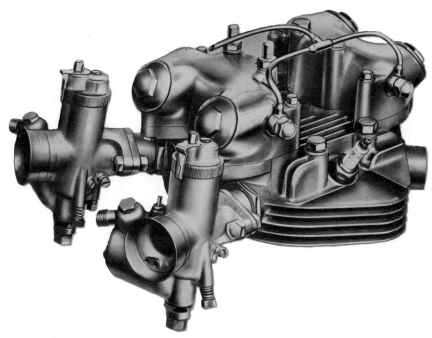

The original twin carburetter splayed port cylinder head first manufactured in 1957 for the 500cc Tiger 100 series models, and at first offered only in kit form

inlet ports of the 650cc Delta heads to make them suitable for the 'souped-up' Thunderbirds, Tiger 110s and the new TR6s they were now tuning.

Rather sadly, the first examples of the Delta heads had been prone to cracking between the holding-down bolts and the valve seats, so for 1958 the combustion spheres were reduced in size which necessitated reshaped piston crowns together with a new range of smaller diameter head inlet and exhaust valves which really was a pity as the engines, perhaps understandably, never seemed to run quite as well afterwards.

However, the twin carburetter 650cc splayed inlet port head was announced in Technical Information Bulletin No.1 (1958 Season's New Features) and appeared in the 1958 Replacement Parts catalogue.

Of all the Service Department technical information bulletins the most popular ever produced was affectionately known as 'Tib-Two', of which thousands were given away. This, we suppose, always accounts for a certain guranteed level of popularity! Tib-Two listed the most advantageous high performance specification for both 500cc and 650cc engines to which any enthusiast, with the aid of Tib-Two, could modify his own machine with the components recommended and depending upon his own skill as a tuner, was able to obtain the maximum power output required for the various types of competitive events in which he wished to partake.

Up to this time the company itself had not built or sold a single machine off the end of the production line in this or even similar condition, nor had such a machine been entered by the company in any competitive events. The Triumph Competition Department at Meriden, inspired and extremely closely monitored by Henry Vale, still worked totally towards ultimate reliability and avoided at all costs spending its time and substance in attempting to achieve road racing status. It was 'off the road', and in scrambles and trials, that durability counted and this was the only quest, and resulted in almost perpetual success in these events.

Triumph Experimental Department dynamometer test bed circa 1958/60. The concrete base of the bed was resiliently rubber mounted and the chamber and exhaust ducting fully sound proofed. Cooling airspeed could be controlled to equate to the equivalent road speed

There were always those who itched to be allowed to 'officially' have a go, knowing the potential power lurking there ready to be developed. Again, but unofficially this time, there were engines being quietly and carefully assembled in dark corners within the Meriden works, with pistons that had strangely shaped crowns, giving hitherto unheard of compression ratios, valve springs and camshafts smuggled in from America, and on the occasions when the 'coast was clear', test beds which again rang with raucous resonances of dynos giving readings never before achieved in the bowels of the test house cellars. The rumours of incredible rpm and bhp figures went round the drawing office and factory floor like wildfire. As before, Edward Turner would be away on business, and the other directors always seemed to be otherwise deeply engaged in some other very important tête-à-tête to the exclusion of all else, that they did not seem to notice. But they always did seem to know of the results if they proved to be worthwhile!

It was therefore inevitable that hovering somewhere in the immediate future was the potential 'world beater' motorcycle which would prove to be the culmination of all the know-how, enthusiasm and the essential Triumph panache that had sustained and matured the breed up to this date and had secured its continuity in the commercial world of the future.

In 1958 the newly devloped 350cc unit construction twin with full rear enclosure was introduced, designated the model 21. The reason behind this designation was to confirm the introduction of a new 21 cubic inch model and to celebrate and commemorate the 21st birthday of the Triumph Engineering Company.

It was later in 1958, when the 1959 sales catalogue had already been printed ready for the Earls Court Show in November, and the 1959 models were actually moving along the production line, being stockpiled for delivery immediately after the show, that 'The Decision' was made.

The 650cc twin carburetter splayed port head engine, developed and supplied in 1958 for use in a Bensen Gyrocopter in Norway. Similar units flew successfully in Finland in 1959

THE BIRTH OF THE BONNIE

Up until 1958, the 650cc engine had been equipped with what had been known as the three-piece crankshaft assembly similar to that which had been used in the original 500cc engine and from which the 650cc had grown. This consisted of two crank-halves attached to each other by 6 x ¼ inch diameter bolts. These bolts also passed through a cast flywheel sandwiching it between the flanges of the crank-halves. Alignment and balancing took place after the three components had been assembled.

However, even though the shanks of the bolts were accurately ground to size and the holes in the crank flanges and flywheel through which they passed were carefully reamed to size, difficulty was encountered in maintaining crankshaft stability under the power outputs to which it was now being subjected. In consequence by March 1958 a crankshaft manufactured from a single forging was nearing the completion of its test programme in readiness for introduction into the 1959 models. This one-piece forging incorporated both crankshaft halves, and a ground central diameter which accepted the centrally mounted cast-iron flywheel. The flywheel was fed over the timing side crank and located on the ground centre diameter of the crankshaft and was finally held in position by three 7/16 inch diameter bolts which passed through the outer periphery of the flywheel into threaded holes located in the crankshaft forging itself.

Experimental Instruction Sheet 419 dated 19th March 1958 listed test bench results of a T110 engine with splayed port head, twin type 6 carburetters, E3134 camshaft and 8.5:1 compression ratio pistons. A flexibly mounted float chamber had been used and the best power of the day was 48.80 bhp (corrected) on a 1¾ inch diameter exhaust pipe system. The engine had been stripped for examination after the test, and passed inspection with flying colours, no fault being found. The remarks column of the instruction sheet reported cryptically that 'Mr Turner expressed satisfaction'. Under the subsequent section headed Further Instructions, experimental manager Frank Baker was detailed to rebuild the engine and install it into the frame of the high speed T110 machine for test at the Motor Industries Research Association (MIRA for short) high speed test track at Lindley near Nuneaton. Even then no one knew that it would turn out to be the Bonnie!

Frank Baker, who had been for many years actively engaged in the high speed motorcycling game, and having joined the firm in 1938 straight from Brooklands where he had prepared record breakers for Noel Pope and others, was an eager and expert engine builder who knew very well the potential of this impending combination and sensed the commecial value of such an enterprise. Consequently, he made sure that the MIRA test sessions were successful. In the wake of the track tests, similar machines were built and subjected to thousands of normal road miles by his experimental testers, led by Percy Tait. This rigorous testing brought to light the need for a little more development on various components which wouldn't, or couldn't, stand the pressures put upon them by the increased power pumped out by the 'twin carburetter T110' as it was known in the department.

By May 1958 notes were passing between the experimental and design departments indicating that the twin carburetter T110 was developing 964 pound inches of torque against the standard T110's 850 and as the T110 six plate clutch of the day could carry only 1,005, things were already getting a little too close for comfort!

The writer recalls being summoned one day late in August 1958, together with other engineering and sales types, to that 'Holy of Holies', the Experimental Shop by Nan Plant, Mr Turner's faithful and long suffering secretary. It was Nan upon whom everyone depended and relied to explain our case, defend our cause, protect our brief or even, prepare us for our doom – and much she bore on our behalf. On this day there was anticipation in the air. Inside the shop stood Edward, one foot resting on a nearby

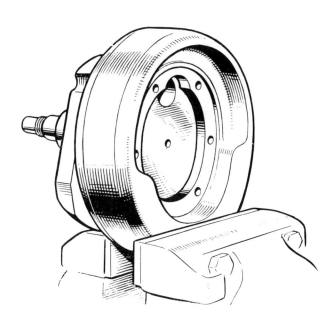

CONNECTING ROD.
BOLT STRETCH
.004-.005 in.
(.102-.127 mm.)

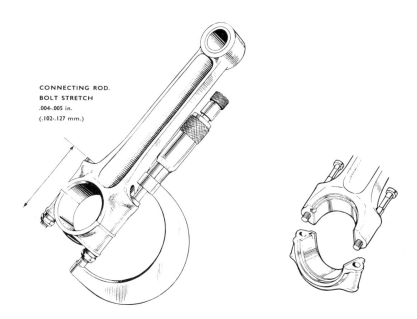

The three piece crankshaft. This crankshaft assembly comprised two crank flange journal and shaft assemblies bolted together with six ground high tensile bolts to sandwich a central cast iron flywheel assembly

37

The one-piece forged crankshaft assembly over which the cast iron flywheel was assembled, and centrally bolted to the crankshaft itself

motorcycle workbench, wearing a light blue American lightweight suit, saying in a stage whisper to Frank Baker (which we were all intended to hear), 'This, my boy, will lead us straight into Carey Street'. The object of his apparent derision was a very smart dark blue and grey two-tone finished twin carburetter T110 (what else could it be called?) with short racing style handlebars protruding from under a shiny black instrument nacelle unit.

As always, Edward had already decided the outcome of the meeting before it had actually been convened, never mind assembled! 'Yes, it has been costed up' confirmed Bud Parker, 'No! we haven't yet worked out the UK or USA retail'. Frank Baker then confirmed that it weighed 404lb and 'Percy Tait could get 128 mph out of it on the electronic timing strip at MIRA, but had one hell of a job to pull up before he reached the banking'. But, one word from those darned Americans, Bill Johnson and his henchman Wilbur Ceder from the West Coast (who for once were both awake at the same time!) and Denis McCormack from the East Coast, and it was 'in'. The name was readily agreed, and in honour of Johnny Allen's achievements at Bonneville Salt Flats in September 1956, it would be the Bonneville.

Although details of the intended 1959 programme and specifications had been given to Production Control in August on Short Order 42, it had all to be re-vamped, re-written and re-published following the US President's visit and the Experimental Shop meeting.

Issue No. 2 took longer than anticipated to come to fruition. For instance, up to this period the US market had always insisted on smaller fuel tanks, high rise handlebars, twinseats with passenger safety straps for the West Coast, vertical dip headlamp lenses and a number of other minor concessions. From this point onward the East/West divergence and specialisation began and at this particular juncture Triumph Production Control had not the remotest idea what was about to hit them. They soon found out when issue No. 2 was released on the 30th December!

On the 1st September 1958, a retail price list was printed in advance indicating intended prices of the 1959 range of models. The range consisted of T20 Tiger Cub, T20

The First Bonneville. The 1959 model was the only version to appear complete with headlamp nacelle, and only the first series in production were built with touring handlebars, two-level twinseat, tangerine and pearl grey petrol tank and with black oil tank and battery box assembly. Later 1959, and US variants had a sports type narrow (single level) twinseat with grey top and lower rim trim band, lowered sports handle-bars and two-tone Royal Blue/Pearl Grey tank with Pearl Grey battery/tool box assembly

Competition Cub, 3TA Model 21, 5TA Speed Twin, T100A Tiger 100, 6T Thunderbird, T110 Tiger 110, TR6 Trophy and the T120 Bonneville 120 which had been printed as a 500cc model and had been overprinted 'ohv twin 650cc'.

The Bonnie still wasn't too sure that it had at last arrived!

But nevertheless, here was the Bonnie, duly authorised, squeezed into the 1958 Earls Court Show programme at the last minute, a show-stopper if ever there were one, a name to be reckoned with even before the first one was sold and it didn't even feature in the 1959 catalogue!

It really should have been there, its arrival had been inevitable!

Edward's Team : Circa Christmas 1959. Back row *(Left to Right)* Eddie Gough, Purchase Manager; Steve Green, maintenance Manager; Jack Welton, Manager, Sales Department, Allan Magill Works Accountant, Neale (Sid) Shilton Export Manager; Eric Headlam, Southern Sales Representative (and Metropolitan Police Liason); Bill Robertson, USA Sales Manager; Jack Shortland, Spares Manager; Frank Baker, Quality Control; John Brock, Overseas Sales Manager; Reuben Jones, Works Superintendent; Les Mattocks, Production Control; Bill Weston, Production Engineer; Ivor Davies, Publicity Manager; John Nelson, Service Manager

Seated, *(Left to Right)* Jack Wickes, Chief Stylist and Project Engineer; Bob Fearon (visitor from BSA, but recently ex-Triumph Works Director) Charles Grandfield, Chief Engineer; Edward Turner, Managing Director; William Winters, Works Director; Bert Coles, Works Manager

THE EVOLUTION OF THE BONNEVILLE

A detailed breakdown of the specification of the major differences incorporated in the Bonnie is given later in this book, but a brief description of the original 1959 and subsequent models, together with the technical development and problems encountered as the seasons rolled by, was thought by the writer to be an essential element in portraying the history of the Bonneville.

If read in conjunction with the actual specification breakdown and note taken of the listed engine number changes and introduction points, it should prove to be useful to the restorer, interesting to the younger enthusiasts and revive more than a few memories for many ex-Bonnie riders. It may also help to settle the many arguments that inevitably take place whenever the latter meet and the subject comes under discussion.

As previously described, the Bonnie arrived as the result of an inexorable developing theme, aided by 'extra-mural' efforts of enthusiasts within the Meriden works, pressured by insistent lobbying from the USA, and possibly encouraged and allowed by those in command to a greater degree than was appreciated at the time. These elements had been so blended, sifted and the final mixture so assembled, tried, tested that it had been made respectable by Frank Baker and his experimental team in readiness for 1959. A comprehensive range of high performance components were then made available, as had been done some time before for the 500cc T100 model. These included close (and wide) ratio gears, racing camshafts and cam followers (tappets), different diameter exhaust pipes, megaphones (including the reversed cone type), one gallon capacity oil tank (rubber mounted), racing type handlebars, lightweight mudguards, competition number plates, rear-set racing footrests, gear lever and brake pedals. The original Grand Prix tachometer drive gearbox was still available and could still be used by removing the dynamo and utilising its drive mechanism (from the exhaust camshaft pinion).

To enable the racing men to carry out the modifications described in Technical Information Bulletin No. 2 a multiplicity of carburetter adaptors, carburetters, high compression pistons and the three keyway camshaft pinions (for accurate cam timing) continued to be manufactured. Consequently 'home-made Bonnies' materialised. However, the first year of the factory production was not without some teething troubles in service. Flywheel bolt breakage problems were overcome by increasing the interference fit of the flywheel bore and the corresponding spigot diameter of the crankshaft by 0.0025 inch (2½ thousandths of an inch). This necessitated heating the flywheel to 95°C (200°F) prior to assembly (the fitter wearing protective gloves for the handling operation). The early pistons developed a crown collapse and skirt distortion problem when the engine was subjected to hard ridden long runs in high ambient temperatures owing to the subsequent heat saturation condition generated. To eliminate the problem the thickness of the piston crown was increased as far as the die would allow, with a further increase when the die was replaced.

Additional modifications during this first 1959 season included the spot welding of the front mudguard to its centre mounting bridge to prevent cracking of the blade at that point. Longer screws were used to secure the outer primary transmission cover to the inner cover and an additional gearbox adjuster was fitted (remember T120 unit construction didn't arrive until 1963). To overcome a premature wear problem in the gearbox camplate in USA competition events, induction hardening of the periphery was introduced and the clutch sprocket centre bore received similar treatment. A much more robust and trouble free voltage regulator was fitted and the original straight-through T110 type silencers were replaced purely as a result of the first signs of impending legislation to control exhaust note sound levels.

In 1960 the Bonnie had a new frame, the contruction being twin front downtube and was known as the duplex frame. This meant that much of the existing range of high

1961 'Thruxton' Bonneville in racing trim incorporating the 1960 high performance parts. The rider shown here was Jack Simonium from Nairobi, Kenya, Olympic National Hockey Team player, who raced this machine successfully at Thruxton in the 1952 500 mile race

performance extras applicable to the cycle parts of the machine would no longer be suitable. Redesigned footrests, brake pedal etc. were made available before the 1961 racing season began. Naturally, the exisiting range of engine 'goodies' continued to be used. However, a welcome addition to the engine parts was a new tachometer drive kit, Part No. CP 181. This consisted of the complete timing cover in which the tachometer drive gearbox was integrally cast, the gears driven from the exhaust camshaft by means of a slot cut across the face of a new exhaust camshaft pinion retaining nut. This enabled the Bonnie to be raced under the prevailing Production Racing regulations which stated that the dynamo must remain in situ. Also included was a tachometer, drive cable and instrument mounting bracket. A special speedometer was made available for use when the gearbox was fitted with a close ratio gear set, made necessary as the speedometer drive was taken from the gearbox layshaft, as with close ratio gears the layshaft rotational speed differed from that of the standard layshaft, affecting speedo cable drive speed.

Service problems encountered with the 1960 model Bonnie were confined mainly to a very small quantity of downtube breakages on the new frame, particularly in competition events, the fractures occurring immediately beneath the steering head lug. This was taken care of for 1961 by the addition of a lower tank rail similar to that fitted to the earlier single downtube frames used from 1936 (and before) until 1960.

At the same time that the lower tank rail was added, the steering head angle was altered at the request of the USA, to make it more suitable for cross-country riding. This modified version of the new frame no longer suffered downtube failure and proved to be considerably stiffer. This stiffening also affected the sympathetic resonant frequency which had a marked effect on the newly designed petrol tank retaining straps (which began to fracture in almost

European Boxing Champion, Henry Cooper and his brother Jim, seen here trying out the new 1961 model 650cc Triumph Bonneville at the 1960 Golden Jubilee Motorcycle show at Earls Court. The original picture was captioned "Double set of Twins"

epidemic proprtions). It took five variants of design and material before the epidemic was totally cured!

The alteration of resonance was also found to be responsible for a carburation problem, despite the rubber mounting of the float chamber, which was traced to high frequency vibration being transmitted to the carburetter mixing chambers creating misfiring when the engine was subjected to hard acceleration. This was overcome by fitting a brass shroud around the needle jet, where it protruded into the choke of the jet block, avoiding the rich mixture condition caused by aeration of the fuel.

Eventually for 1961 the rubber mounted float chamber was dispensed with and two standard Amal Monobloc carburetters specified. It wasn't long however before racing 'chopped-off' monoblocs appeared, fitted by the racing men, and a return to the rubber mounted remote float chamber became necessary.

Further changes made in 1961 were the incorporation of needle roller bearings for the gearbox layshaft, an oil seal in the oil pressure release valve (tell-tale button shaft), reduction of the overall gear ratios by fitting a 21 tooth engine sprocket, the front and rear brake shoes made fully floating and to suit the magneto ignition system, a lower output A.C. generator stator was fitted. 1961 also saw the introduction of the American T120R (Road) and T120C   43

On the 5th September 1962, at the Bonneville Salt Flats, Utah, a new A.M.A. Motorcycle World Speed Record of 224.57 mph for the Flying Kilo was achieved by a 650cc Triumph Streamliner built and prepared by Joe Dudek, and ridden by Bill Johnson of California. Earlier on the 21st August the same team had achieved the A.M.A's Formula SC (streamlined, using pump gasoline, but no supercharger) record speed of 205.785 miles per hour, and on the 24th August had broken the A.M.A's absolute World Speed Record (Formula SA), using blended fuel, but no supercharger, at 230.269mph

(Competition) models with variations of specification to suit both East and West Coast markets.

For 1962 a wider and consequently heavier flywheel was fitted to the crankshaft, increasing the balance factor from 50% to 71%. This provided greater flywheel inertia which provided the competition models with a better 'bite' when the rear wheel returned to earth after the machine became airborne during American-type T.T. races and moto-cross events.

This advantage was further consolidated when the existing crankshaft, which had straight-sided balance weight cheeks, was replaced with a new component on which the cheeks were pear-shaped. This new crankshaft, together with the heavier flywheel, enabled the balance factor to be increased further to 85%.

Other features for 1962 included the previously mentioned fifth (and final) petrol tank strap, new 'gas tap' type petrol taps, one of which became a reserve. This was the first Bonnie to have such a facility but it proved later to be absolutely essential to have both taps fully open when using maximum performance to avoid fuel starvation. 145 lb/inch Girling rear suspension shock absorber units were fitted, a 140 mph (240 kph) speedometer and the twinseat cover incorporating a grey top. Electrical equipment changes included a new lighting switch, ammeter, rectifier and the deletion of the wiring harness headlamp plug and socket for none other than safety reasons!

In 1963, the Bonnie virtually started again. There were so many alterations that it would be impossible to include them in this brief year by year summary. Therefore, the reader is advised to peruse the 1963 specification which appears elsewhere. Perhaps the greatest change was the transformation of the separate gearbox/engine into the unit construction configuration. The engine, gearbox and primary transmission were contained in a single unit, deleting the magneto in favour of twin contact breaker coil ignition, and with

The 1963 unit-construction 650cc Bonneville incorporating the new combined engine/gearbox/transmission unit

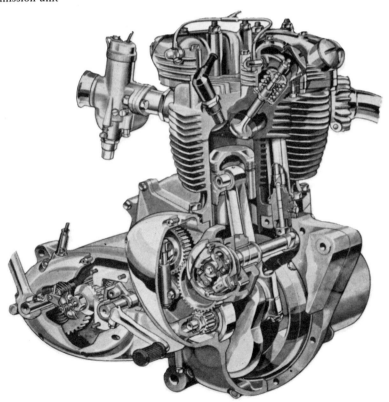

The 1963 integrated engine/gearbox/transmission power unit

a fixed endless duplex chain primary drive. The frame was also drastically altered and became once again the single front downtube type.

With so many changes of specification in one season it was perhaps natural that some problems would be encountered in service. There were, however, relatively few, which were confined principally to the breaking up or granulation of the new clutch centre shock absorber rubbers incorporating ¼ inch holes through their centres to provide additional resilience and flexibility. These were replaced with rubbers made from a softer mix and incorporating chamfered edges because of granulation failure, which were identified by being coloured green.

Two other sporadic problems occurred, the first being difficulty in selecting top gear caused by a slight gear selector quadrant foul condition inside the new unit construction gearbox shell and the second problem was difficulty in locating the nose of the steering lock into the crown stem. Neither of these problems caused quite as much concern as the occasional main bearing failure resulting from the new unit construction crankcase casting being so much stiffer than the previous type, with the consequence that the bearings themselves were subjected to a slightly increased diametral fit under running conditions (or perhaps a less forgiving crankcase than the previous non-unit castings?).

By 1964, the Bonnie had become fully established as the undisputed leader of the competitive array of available high performance motorcycles and whilst, without doubt, the first of the 'super bikes', progressive development continued with specific detailed improvements to increase performance and further consolidate reliability.

Road specification models and competition variants for East and West Coast distribution in the USA began to diverge further in requirements to include the so-called TT version of the competition model. The production of 'UK and general export' Bonnevilles had to be adjusted and scheduled to meet the demands, for in those days the slogan 'Export or Die' still meant what it said. It is also interesting to note that the practice of incorporating into the specification of the standard machine components which had previously appeared only in High Performance parts lists had now begun.

Despite the very successful efforts to improve reliability, problems in service still existed, the major being the failure of drive side main bearings as in the previous year's model, although 3 spot (greater clearance) bearings were now being used to accommodate the increased pre-loading of the bearing when fitted into the stiffer unit construction crankcase.

The introduction of the twin contact breaker, designed to give the best possible ignition conditions (i.e. one contact breaker per cylinder) was found to be the cause of high piston crown temperature problems with consequential skirt siezures, i.e. the individual ignition points setting proved to be quite satisfactory when in brand new condition but when the initial settling down of the fibre contact breaker heels and the cam surface had taken place it proved to be almost impossible to reset correct ignition timing on both cylinders without actually juggling with the points gap, an operation which appeared, and ultimately proved to be, beyond the skill of the average owner/mechanic. Consequently, many Bonnies were run with one cylinder timing spot-on and the other not nearly so, the piston in the 'not quite' cylinder suffering accordingly. Running a machine in this condition also had the effect of increasing the inherent vertical twin vibration, resulting in fractured mudguards, oil tanks, et cetera.

Eventually, later in 1967, a redesigned contact breaker enabled each of the contact breaker points to move independently on the base plate allowing independent adjustment for each of the cylinders. This facility was additional to the overall adjustment of the complete assembly by means of slotted holes in the contact breaker base plate through which passed the fixing screws, which had been the only means of adjustment available in the earlier type.

Nevertheless the problem did indicate that the Bonnie's engine had reached such a

Percy Tait, the well-known motorcycle racer, and, at the time, Triumph Experimental Department Works Tester, aboard his production class racing Bonnie in 1964. Percy was "Mr. Triumph" around the race circuits in Europe and earned that title with consistent results and successes for many·years

high state of tune that a more positive means of finding actual engine top dead centre was essential and provision for stroboscopic timing was now becoming absolutely necessary. A further indication of the increasing load on the engine was the premature wear being exhibited on exhaust camshaft lobes. This latter problem initiated work that was finalised with the introduction of positive lubrication of the cams and cam followers together with a further type of heat treatment and hardening process for the camshafts in 1966.

However, 1965 was to see the introduction of the top dead centre (TDC) location facility. It consisted of a suitably positioned slot in the periphery of the flywheel and a threaded bore situated in the crankcase immediately to the rear of the cylinder block face. To establish TDC, a hexagonal-headed plug was removed from the crankcase threaded hole and replaced by a threaded sleeve through which a pin was inserted, the nose of the pin locating in the slot in the flywheel at TDC exactly. This system continued to be used, although it was decided in 1965 that it would be more important to set the engine at its fully advanced position (38° before TDC) when carrying out the ignition timing operation utilising the new electronic timing meter equipment from a transducer pulsed from the 38° slot.

Other detailed refinements, some like the TDC facility a direct outcome of problems experienced in service, were incorporated in 1965 models, but the majority were introduced as part of the continual attempt to achieve improvements in the performance and overall reliability. The increase in divergence between the UK general export, USA East and West Coast models continued. The West Coast were also pressing for a more sophisticated specification for the TT model which had been developed directly as a result of the need to be successful in Californian competitive events, in particular the prominent Ascot TT race circuit in Los Angeles.

This year (1965) and this year only in the Bonnie's life, the crankshaft location was transferred from the timing RH side to the drive side. This was achieved by utilising a new crankshaft timing pinion which butted up to the outer face of the crankshaft main bearing   47

1965 650cc T120C West Coast 'TT' Competition Model. This model dominated the USA West Coast speed record books and had won more USA type 'TT' competition races than all other makes combined at that time

journal instead of the inner spool of the bearing itself. The engine drive sprocket was altered and instead of butting up to the end of the crankshaft splines, it butted up to the inner spool of the drive side bearing, therefore reversing the previous arrangement. The envisaged advantages of the new arrangement were a more positive primary chain alignment (which was not eminently consistent under the previous positioning of the sprocket) and a controlled loading of the crankshaft drive side bearing which remained prone to sporadic premature failure.

Rapport now existed between the Meriden factory and the USA distributors on both Coasts which could only be described as unique in the motorcycling world. This close liaison was responsible for initiating many exploratory developments carried out at the factory. They were the direct results of the distributors' and their individual dealers' deep and intensive involvement in sales and service activities coupled with the participation in competitive events, the objectives being to uphold their success and maintain their leadership in the market. Added to this was the constant drive towards improving maintenance facilities and the simplification of servicing procedures.

The technical interchange was considerable and, more often than not, extremely fruitful and had not yet reached a state where the 'tail was wagging the dog'. The entire factory/distributor relationship, not only with the USA but throughout the world, was totally dedicated to 'improving the breed' and maintaining the number one position in the big bike field. This annual search for increased performance, whether it was in the 0 to 60 mph or 0 to 100 mph range, or simply to find another elusive horsepower to squeeze out of the engine, often meant the incorporation of the previously developed high performance 'goodies' into the standard catalogue model. This philosophy, without doubt, had resulted in the power characteristics of the road-going Bonnie becoming somewhat more brittle than before and much more than many normal road-going riders came to care for. In view of this it was often

Best wishes always John. Bob Leppan

Still further world speed records achieved by Triumph!

The team of Robert Blueflodt, Alexis Tremulus and Bob Leppan were to make many very successful visits from Michigan to the Bonneville Salt Flats in Utah with the Gyronaut X-1 Streamliner. Following their shattering of the A.M.A. World Speed Record by achieving 245.667mph in August 1966, Bob Leppan later broke his own world record again at 247.763mph, culminating then in his ultimate run of 264.437mph on the 20th October 1970. Further confirming his triumphant claim to the title of "The World's Fastest Motorcyclist from 1966 through to 1974." The Gyronaut X-1 was powered by two 650cc Triumph engines in tandem and was 13 feet long, 3ft. 3 in. wide and only 2ft. 8 in. tall

the practice at the factory Service Department repair shop to solve a customer's 'unsolvable vibration problem by rebuilding his engine using 'gentler' camshafts, closer fitting pistons with a lower compression ratio, a gearbox sprocket which allowed a lower overall gear ratio and other 'secret' modifications, to finish up with a much sweeter but almost equally attractive performance machine, together with a satisfied customer.

By this time there was a heartfelt feeling growing amongst many at Meriden that the amount and type of horsepower being built into the standard over-the-counter Bonnie was more than enough and had transformed it from a high speed tourer into nothing short of a production racer in disguise. It seemed that unless the remainder of the high performance parts were fitted and the bike used as such, the excess power was somehow being inwardly absorbed, creating a form of indigestion which manifested itself in premature fatigue and failure. Be that as it may, plans were already in motion to break through the further available power and performance barrier for 1966.

These plans included a higher compression ratio (9 : 1) and a change of valve springs. The springs were not new but had been designed originally for the 6T model Thunderbird when it had camshafts which incorporated quietening ramp cam forms. The Experimental Department had discovered that they provided a most satisfactory surge and a bounce free operation when fitted to the Bonnie. A change of flywheel was made, the new one being 2½ lb lighter, but its shape enabled the 85% balance factor to be retained. As previously mentioned, the crankshaft location reverted to the timing side and the exhaust camshafts received their much needed positive lubrication. A heavy duty single lipped roller bearing replaced the overworked ball bearing on the crankshaft drive side main journal. A new single leading shoe front brake also appeared in 1966 which demanded much more respect from   49 riders who were used to the previous model's brake as the later shoes gave more than 40% increase in friction area.

A mid-season modification which had been unobtrusively slipped in was a change of material used for the exhaust pipe adaptor sleeves in the cylinder head from steel to aluminium. The steel sleeves had become prone to loosening in the head and it was considered that the closer coefficient of expansion that the sluminium sleeves would provide with the alloy cylinder head might improve matters. Alas, this was not to be. It was soon discovered that when the clip which secured the exhaust pipe to the sleeve was tightened, it had a collapsing effect. Consequently, the threads on the sleeve became undersize and loose from that moment, defeating the whole object of the change. Needless to say, a return to steel sleeves was made as soon as possible.

The 1967 season saw fewer technical changes than any previous year, a major part of the work of the Experimental Department having been directed towards consolidating the existing design. Even so, uncertainty was beginning to be felt by the technical decision makers of the Bonnie, and it was true to say that the autonomy of Meriden and the control of its own destiny began to be eroded at this time. For example, 1967 was the first season where the compilation and publication of the Triumph catalogue was transferred from Meriden to BSA headquarters at Small Heath, Birmingham.

Another move which strengthened the feeling of foreboding which was running through all departments at Meriden was the establishment of a Divisional Research and Development Centre in an old country mansion called Umberslade Hall situated at Hockley Heath on the southern outskirts of Birmingham. It was obvious that the seeds of 'integration' had been planted. Whether or not Umberslade Hall could ever have been scheduled at any time during its previous existence as a 'folly' has not been established, but the formation of a motorcycle Research and Development Centre within its portals could in retrospect probably be so described.

It was, although not planned, to bring some light relief to Meriden during the dark years which followed, brought about by the fact that it took so long for any action to emanate from their efforts. This, coupled with the description of the idyllic location which began to filter back to Meriden of its sylvan setting, with peacocks strutting in the grounds, soon led to its becoming known as 'Slumberglade' Hall.

However, 'Slumberglade' became 'Disneyland' when the results did eventually start to arrive at the production lines of both Triumph and BSA.

But we digress. The actual test and development work on the Bonnie continued to be undertaken at Meriden, although the procurement of production materials soon began to be directed to the centralised Purchase Department based at BSA, Small Heath. The new rules on buying were that, if the Small Heath department could procure components at a cheaper price or even an identical price, the purchase should be transferred to Small Heath. If the component required could be interchanged with the equivalent BSA motorcycle part, then it should be purchased by the centralised organisation. In other words purchasing had been taken over too. No one had yet envisaged where this would eventually lead to.

But back to Bonnie. As we have said, no great changes took place in 1967 and various models continued unchanged except for some internal improvements. These included a switch to pistons manufactured by Messrs. Hepworth and Grandage (Hepolite), as prior to this time Meriden had always made their own pistons. The connecting rod was strengthened and the oil pump had its scavenge capacity increased to overcome a condition termed 'wet sumping' (once described in a telex from the USA as 'Wet something'!). Wet sumping only occurred when the engine had been subjected to a relatively long period of full bore running, and the pump had found difficulty in returning oil from the crankcase to the tank quickly enough to prevent smoking exhausts. Alterations were also made to the exhaust cam/tappet positive lubrication system, both problems not being entirely unconnected with the recent introduction of the latest multigrade high detergent oils. 1967 was also to see the last of the USA West Coast T120C TT model.

The slogan which appeared on the 1968 catalogue was 'Precision, Power and Performance' and certainly the competition successes achieved throughout the world during the previous twelve months augured well for the approaching season. The additional power being squeezed out of the engine had created the problems of camshaft wear, piston crown distortion and tingling vibration. At the same time legislation in many countries was beginning to take its toll of the power manufactured at the input end, by strangulation from the use of more effective silencers at the other, to achieve requisite noise levels.

However, these setbacks were only regarded by Meriden as problems to be overcome and the Development Department, at this juncture still located at Meriden, continued to strive to maintain and uphold the claim (also made in the '68 catalogue), 'surely the most potent, fully equipped road machine in standard production today'. That is, that part of the department that wasn't already engaged in racing activities!

Doug Hele and Bert Hopwood still steadfastly refused to leave their Meriden domicile and to set up their technical camp at the BSA Group Research and Development Centre at Umberslade Hall. The staff who were already there were gradually forming up and beginning to show an interest in the technical future of the Motorcycle Division. Whether or not the Bonneville was planned to be included in this future we shall see.

Nevertheless,, further changes took place in the Bonnie in 1968 although not necessarily outwardly visible. Increasing acceptance by British industry of UNF threads, to replace the long used British Standards, meant that tooling costs at Meriden were rising prohibitively and the economists' decision was thus taken to accept the trend as quickly as possible. Consequently, this immediately produced a new range of components as far as part numbers and interchangeability was concerned. For example, one of the first effects of the change-over resulted in the initial series of the newly developed shuttle valve front forks utilising the old CEI threads with UNF equivalents introduced shortly afterwards.

The new Lucas 6CA contact breaker base plate was introduced at this time. This at last provided the facility enabling both sets of ignition contact breaker points to be positioned and set individually, thus giving far more accurate ignition timing on both cylinders than had ever been possible with the 4CA fixed points type.

The previously described TDC location system, which had been introduced in 1965 had, by now, proved its worth in service and the production departments had begun taking advantage of it by first using the facility with the stroboscope to finally check ignition settings after each machine had completed its 'rolling road' test prior to despatch. However, it was felt that it could be used to more effect if a more sophisticated type of electronic indicator than the normal strobe light could be utilised. By installing a plug-in transducer into the crankcase TDC location hole, the transducer wired to an electronic ignition timing degree indicator, it became possible to adjust each set of points separately and accurately in the all-important fully advanced position with the engine running. The transducer picked up its impulses from the slot machined in the flywheel at a position chosen to ensure that the pistons would be 38° BTDC when the impulse 'hit the dial'. To avoid confusion this 38° slot was machined well away from the existing TDC hole in the flywheel which resulted in the location hole in the crankcase being moved from the top (behind the cylinder block of the crankcase) to just below the forward engine mounting.

This arrangement unfortunately proved impractical in use, so by popular request the Design Department soon re-instituted the location in its original position, amended the flywheel slot accordingly and discontinued the front access hole completely.

Ultimately, the TDC hole in the flywheel was eliminated and the 38° slot was standardized. At this stage the service and parts departments were dealing with three conditions of crankcase and four conditions of flywheel! Nevertheless, the final result of all

Malcolm Uphill's visit to Meriden in 1969 following his Isle of Man success in winning the Production TT Race that year. His Bonnie was the first production motorcycle ever to lap the island circuit at over 100mph (Triumph Bonneville's were also 3rd, 5th and 6th in this event). Bonnevilles also won the Barcelona 24 hour race, the Swedish Grand Prix and the Thruxton 500 mile GP that year with Triumphs in 2nd, 5th, 6th and 7th places. In this photograph (*Left to Right*) are Jim Munday, Bert Hopwood, John Walford, Malcolm Uphill, Norman Hyde, Doug Hele, Allan Magill, Bob Haines and Tony Mayhew (Champion)

this hole/slot juggling was that the ignition setting and timing on each and every machine was henceforth more accurately and precisely set at the factory than had been hitherto possible using a stroboscope, and usually was not disturbed or upset by human hand until the first 500 mile service!

In 1969 the slogan on the catalogue changed but the Bonnie hardly did at all. The home catalogue proclaimed 'top line for '69', the American version persuaded the respective customer to 'leave it all behind on a Triumph '69' and then portrayed the models in the range as viewed through rainbow-hued cross hatch lenses, which ensured that any of the technical features described in the text were not in the least discernible in the photographs! Perhaps this was not without reason as the visual changes in '69 were at an all-time low and design introductions were minimal except for the continuing process of 'unification of the threaded components'!

The Bonnie was now at the pinnacle of its achievements, its field problems were few and its reputation high. Apart from its basic inherent twin cylinder vibration problems, it was still the 'epitome of achievement in motorcycle ownership for more motorcyclists than could ever afford to buy one. You were no one if you didn't ride a Bonnie!

Even so, it was becoming longer in the tooth and dealers were beginning to glance over their shoulders at the encroaching competition. True, the three-cylinder Trident had been announced and released but a replacement for the Bonnie, or at least a brand new version, was long awaited.

The P39 model was known to be 'on the stocks' at Umberslade and this knowledge alone had a definite retarding effect on any remedial action being taken to improve the current model in service. In fact, not a single action to rectify any field problem was authorised unless it could be shown that a financial saving would be made by carrying out the necessary modification.

All very laudable, one might say, unless as a new Triumph owner one's own camshafts had become worn out, or one's main bearings had failed just outside the warranty period! However, the order of the day was 'to tighten one's belt and live off one's fat'. The real tragedy was that by this time most of the original design team had been transferred from Meriden to join the increasing throng at Umberslade Hall, and those who had been left at Meriden to 'keep the drawings tidy' were in a totally non-executive role. Nevertheless, they were a few brave souls who realised that unless clandestine, unauthorised rectification actions (just like the old days) were not taken immediately on the production line there would be no future for the new design, whatever it might be or whenever it arrived. It must be understood that, at this time, cost effective administration had reached such a stage that any modification, regardless of its urgency or importance, had to be submitted to the next monthly Service Meeting. Any decision taken there would be referred to the next month's Finance Committee Meeting. This committee would then refer the decision back to the next month's Design Department Meeting, *ad infinitum*!

Thus the inevitable 'us and them' syndrome started. Those who were regarded as 'them', designing and developing for the planned future, thus appeared oblivious of the current problems out in the field and indeed often continuing to re-incorporate the very causes of these problems into the new models. At the same time those who remained at the factory, regarding themselves as 'us', continually strove to keep the production track operating and above all, as far as they were concerned, endeavoured to maintain the reputation for reliability which had always been the key to the world wide success the Triumph Company had enjoyed. This was a fact of which the 'Meriden crowd' were well aware.

The actual technical changes and improvements for 1969 were the completion of change-over to UNF threads on the engine/gearbox unit, the introduction of nitride hardened camshafts, which finally eliminated the problem of cam lobe wear, the fitting of the latest vibration-proof encapsulated alternator stator and the exhaust pipes coupled together with a cross-over tube to aid power increase and soften exhaust note. A new pushrod cover tube design was incorporated which almost proved to be a 'débâcle'. The 'powers that be' also decided that gears and shafts used in the Bonnie gearbox that were common with the gearbox of the new three-cylinder Trident would, in future, be manufactured at the Small Heath factory where the Trident engine/gearbox units were being assembled. This move also turned out to be the basis for a further production disaster, as it resulted in the basic dimensions of the parts concerned being altered after something like thirty years of manufacture!

Instead of amending the drawings as Meriden should have done years previously, and putting them in line with the many years of proven and accepted practice, it was decided that the parts to be manufactured at Small Heath must be finished to the *original* drawings. The result of this decision was a complete new range of shafts and gears with diameters and bores differing by just a few ten-thousandths of an inch from the existing Meriden production components. This meant that the 'new' parts had to be given a 'new' series of part numbers to obviate confusion with each other thus avoiding a mis-match condition which could have been disastrous in the gearbox.

How much more simple and less expensive it would have been to have amended the dimensions on the drawings in line with the long existing shop floor custom and practice, born out of good old-fashioned know-how. Yes, Meriden was now beginning to feel the   53 burden of remote divisionalisation.

There will always be those who say that 1970 was the last year of the genuine Bonnie. For it was to be next year, in 1971, that the Umberslade design concept was planned to emerge in the form of the existing engine/gearbox unit housed in a new frame. In reality this was to mean that what little design effort had been directed towards the solving of day to day service and production problems with the existing models resulted in remarkably few technical changes and improvements actually being incorporated in the 1970 model.

This was not necessarily because the Sales Department really believed the USA publicity hand-out which stated that the Bonnie was 'the standard by which all others are judged' or even that you may be 'man enough for a Triumph' as the chosen slogan used on the UK posters stated, but because the overall financial situation had now reached the point where any expenditure had to be solely reserved for those models being developed and destined for appearance in 1971.

However, another new colour and a modicum of technical change did allow the 1970 series to be called a new season's model, although each new feature was hard won and introduced solely to overcome production and field problems, rather than being the results of the stylist's pen.

It was reported that the design and development effort at Umberslade was being concentrated on the P39 model, eventually destined, it was believed, to use both the Triumph and BSA power units, although the prototypes were rarely seen at Meriden. In fact, at this point the once very active Triumph Development Department at Meriden, under the control of Bert Hopwood and run by Doug Hele, had ceased to maintain a direct interest in the twin cylinder models and was steadily progressing towards becoming a three-cylinder Trident racing shop.

It had been planned that 1971 was to be the year when the long heralded design achievements of the Research and Development Department at Umberslade Hall, on which the Motor Cycle Division relied to rescue the situation, were to be released to the waiting world; the year when the faith of the big banks supporting the group's massive overdrafts was to be justified and the new generation of motorcycles, born of what was claimed to be fresh and fundamental market research nurtured by 'fresh look' engineering expertise, was finally to be presented to the public and the much awaited new generation of Bonnies would be released.

This presentation of the entirely new combined 16 model range for both Triumph and BSA was executed in truly mammoth proportions and regal splendour. Few who were privileged to be present at the launch at The Royal Lancaster Hotel on that October day in 1970 will ever forget the lavish and flowing hospitality. The memorable luncheon and dinner, the distributors and dealers who came from all over the world and the notable and distinguished guests from Government and Civil high offices.

The evening's entertainment was both significant and symbolic, from comedian Dave Allen to the Younger Generation dancers, culminating in a scintillating unveiling and presentation of the 16 models in turn, each wall-mounted in its own massive three-dimensional picture frame, under intense spotlight illumination accompanied by a fanfare of trumpets and a professional commentary. The whole effort was an undeniable advertising and public relations success.

Even so, there were those present who knew the motorcycle business more than intimately and who expressed doubts. Among them was John Y. Sangster. There were others present who were fully aware that the factory production departments had not yet even seen the drawings, let alone had been able to make the tools, jigs and fixtures necessary to enable production of the Bonneville to recommence.

In order to keep the Triumph plant working, Tiger 100 models were rushed forward out of normal sequence into the build programme.

The Triumph factory 'Mecca' to many and home of the Bonneville, at Meriden in the heart of Warwickshire, near Coventry. Soon to become the scene of a bitter and prolonged struggle for survival . . .

The drawings still didn't appear during September or October, by which time no more Tiger 100 models could possibly be scheduled resulting from the fact that the total annual Tiger 100 components had been consumed, and there were no further components with which to build them. Bonneville and Trophy engine/gearbox units were built, tested and stacked wherever there was space. What was known as the 'Big Wait' started as there were still no frames in which to install the engine units.

Production assembly workers were kept standing by, fully paid and ready to go, for over three months. To counter the inevitable boredom a new and surprising talent was rapidly discovered amongst them. That of playing chess! It transpired that some superb battles took place using chequer boards marked out on the tops of packing cases with all manner of exotic chessmen, oil pumps for pawns, valve springs for queens and rockers for rooks et cetera. 'Tournaments' reigned supreme.

The resentment of all at Meriden at being prevented from producing anything for weeks on end was enormous. The stories of Umberslade's inability to get things right were legion and oft confirmed by the fact that no fewer than 1,200 modifications were made before the final drawings eventually emerged! Nevertheless the awaited drawings did finally appear under the generic and, as far as the Meriden workforce were concerned, foreign title of Model P39, and all hell was let loose on the shop floor as the now frustrated workers threw themselves into the highly belated but mammoth task of producing the jigs, equipment and tools, at the same time sorting out production procedures necessary to get the new Bonnie on to the assembly track as quickly as possible in an effort to get back to work and to reverse the effect of three months loss of production and profit that had been endured on the company. Obviously, all knew that no amount of effort could possibly regain the total loss caused by holding the complete factory's assembly teams on three months paid stand-by.

On the 25th November in the midst of this endeavour to recover, the Group   55

Managing Director invited all the Meriden employees to a meeting to be held in the works canteen. They expected to learn at last the reasons for the Motorcycle Division's three months complete production standstill. One can imagine the incredulous looks developing on the worker's faces when they heard that the meeting had been convened solely to inform them that any demands for wage increases would have to be moderated as any such increases 'could not be granted for nothing' and 'there can only be more money if we are more productive, otherwise the factory will be closed down!' The trade union convenors and stewards, having been given prior notice of the meeting's agenda, refused to accept the statement and declined to attend. On top of this, when the first P39 frame was finally completed it was discovered that the Bonneville engine could not be installed into it!

After several attempts it was found that the only means of fitting the engine was to remove the rocker boxes, the only snag being that it was impossible then to refit them once the engine had been located in the frame. What little regard remained at Meriden for Umberslade and all that it signified at this point finally disappeared, never to return and perhaps understandably so! Eighteen modifications to the long-proven arrangements for the fitting of the Triumph twin cylinder rocker boxes had to be made. The modifications included amendment to cylinder head, rocker boxes themselves, studs, bolts and gaskets and were left to be initiated and brought to production fruition by Meriden's staff itself. These home-spun modifications finally allowed production of the Bonnie to recommence just prior to Christmas 1970. However, it was now firmly believed at Meriden (and had it not now been shown?) that it had never been intended that the Triumph P39 version of the Bonneville should ever be allowed to see the light of day. This then was the conclusion engendered by three months of total inactivity at the factory, and believed by all to be fully justified in this final result.

Much could be said of the first year's experience with this 1971 model, suffice it to say that unless the rider was at least over 6 feet tall, with a minimum inside leg measurement of 32 inch, he was very likely to fall off the machine when coming to a halt, unless he had previously selected and headed for the safety of a high kerb-stone!

The report compiled by Triumph service representative Stan Truslove, who just happened to be 6 feet 4 inches tall with a 34 inch inside leg measurement, after a tour of Triumph dealers throughout France in April 1971, indicated that most of his time was spent attempting to convince all he met that he himself had not designed the bike or had even been the model around (or under) which it had been designed!

In an effort to reduce the saddle height no less than three frame variations were introduced in the first year, none of which were readily interchangeable and even included the addition of a thinner twinseat. When the height problem was reported to Umberslade, their tart retort was 'if the frames had been built to drawing, they would be alright'. This remark incensed the Meriden Inspection Department who, having immediately taken a frame from production and subjected it to totally critical inspection, reported that it was indeed taller than the actual drawing called for by twenty eight thousandths of an inch!

But the new Bonnie was comfortable and, above all, it did steer very well. Engine vibration was more noticeable, probably because of the return to a twin front downtube 'tuning fork' frame design (shades of 1960/1/2?). Nevertheless, it did sell, although not particularly well, whereas the BSA variant with the frame in grey painted finish lost sales with alarming rapidity.

Sadly, the New Generation lavishly launched for 1971 was not to prove the scintillating yet desperate prerequisite for solving the group's financial situation, but to be an even more rapid vehicle on which the Motorcycle Division began its accelerating downhill slide. Eventually, by the end of the season (July 31st 1971) an official trading deficit of nearly 2.5 millions was announced as a result of which the BSA shares fell from a 1971 high of 87 pence each to 37 pence.

The 1971 Model T120R – 4-Speed USA model

So it was in July 1971, a month prior to the official commencement of the 1972 model season, the announcement was made of the Board of Directors' intention to reduce the workforce at Small Heath, Umberslade Hall and Meriden.

It was also announced during July that a company known as Vision Enterprises Ltd had approached the Board with a view to offering £5½ million for not less than 50% (and not more than 60%) of the share capital of the group. It was also revealed that there were other parties interested in a similar move, amongst them the giant Tube Investment Group and the Austrian cycle, moped and motorcycle firm of Steyr-Daimler-Puch. However these 'things that might have been' were held up while both BSA and Vision Enterprises awaited the outcome of an investigation into, and appraisal of, BSA's financial situation and future prospects being carried out by the firm of auditors, Messrs. Coopers and Lybrand.

On August 3rd the *Daily Express* confirmed that Vision Enterprises were no longer interested and not prepared to make a bid of 55 pence per share as had been suggested. No doubt this decision had been reached when BSA had revealed that it was anticipating a £3 million loss that year, with a further £1 million deficit due to the cost of divisional rationalisation.

By November 1st a 'Company Doctor', Mr Brian Eustace, had been appointed to the BSA main Board of Directors as Chief Executive; Eric Turner, until then Chairman of the Board, staying on in an advisory capacity. At the extraordinary General Meeting held on that day, it was announced that the overall trading loss of the Motorcycle Division had amounted to over £8 million. The shares fell to an all-time low of 7½ pence. A London columnist at that time commented that 'BSA had managed to snatch disaster from the jaws of success!'

Talks had already been initiated with the Government's Department of Trade and   57

The 1971 Model T120 R – 4-Speed home model. It has the Tiger Gold mudguards and fuel tank with Black lining and stripes, plus White pin-stripes

Industry in an attempt to find a solution to BSA's financial difficulties but it was estimated that £20 million would be required if the company were to be financed adequately and safely into the 1972 season. The banks would only lend £10 million.

If no financial help could be obtained from the Government (and it was not to be) the only solution Eric Turner was able to offer was to begin negotiations to close down the Small Heath works, with the inevitable redundancy of its 3,000 employees, and to concentrate motorcycle production at Meriden 'as Triumph is a small, self-contained unit with much lower overheads'. This was an important statement, as far as the survival of the Bonnie was concerned, but was often apparently forgotten or pushed aside in the many arguments yet to come. In January 1972 the Research and Development Centre, Umberslade Hall, was finally closed down and selected personnel and equipment transferred over to Meriden. The half year's trading figures announced on January 28th revealed a further trading loss of £1.5 million, with an unlikely 'break-even' announced, even at the end of the year.

However, by March 1972 production of the commercially ill-conceived Ariel Tricycle (no mean contributor to the company's ultimate collapse) was rushing towards its inevitable end and the redundancies forecast by Eric Turner had taken place. Lord Shawcross had, in November 1971, become interim Chairman of the Board and it was reported that he had announced that both BSA and Triumph big bikes were to be produced at Meriden with the new 350cc range shelved and the proposed 250cc range dropped altogether. History shows that the 350s were never to materialise. In actual fact these plans, like many others, were not adhered to and limited numbers of 500, 650 and 750cc BSA models, together with the Triumph Trident three-cylinder engine unit, continued to be produced with approximately 1,100 employees retained at the Small Heath works. There were, however, a small number of Meriden built police machines (TR6P models) which were fitted with BSA petrol tank badges, for the export market. The 500cc Tiger 100, 650cc TR6 model Trophy and the T120 Bonnie survived at Meriden but it was a bitter and uneasy partnership between Meriden and headquarters.

The American organisation for BSA/Triumph was by now controlled by a completely new and recently superimposed heirarchy. Based at Verona, New Jersey it now embarked on an 'all-out, no holds barred' (or expenses spared) advertising and PR exercise in an effort to 58 dispose of their accumulated Umberslade design stock. Nevertheless, despite these efforts,

The 1972 Model T120 RV – 5-Speed UK and general export model. Detailed changes included a lowered frame and re-designed seat together with shortened front forks providing a lower seating and riding position than the previous year's model. Further frame, air box and seat changes were made during the 1972 season to lower the rider position yet further

which included taking advertising space in the glossy male (and female) magazines, it soon became increasingly, and painfully obvious that you 'can't sell a product the customers don't like'. So much for the new generation and informed market research.

Suffice it to say, the Bonnie only just survived this period of chaos, probably on its past glories and reputation, but even more probably on the loyalty of the Overseas Distribution staff and dealer network. This loyalty never appears to count for much in the eyes of modern big business consultants, but is more valuable than is realised to a long established family business which had been built up on the basis of trust between the supplier, dealer and customer.

Once again, back to the Bonneville.

For 1972 the major modification was the introduction of the reduced height frame but other problems were experienced. These frames fractured and oil leaked from the spine tube oil tank, centre stands collaped (often taking the frames with them), the front forks continued to leak oil and the engine vibration was still painfully obvious and the main bearing failure now of predictable regularity. Other than the changes listed in the specification sheet in the technical section of this book, the 1972 Bonnie continued almost unmodified from the original Umberslade model introduced in 1971.

Some progressive evolution of the Bonnie continued and by far the most important single change in August 1972 for the 1973 models, was the introduction of the 750cc engine. The first series to be manufactured were of 724cc with a bore and stroke ratio of 75 x 82 mm, the second series had a capacity of 747cc with a 76 x 82 mm bore and stroke. This larger engine was introduced after only four months of producing the smaller version. Although of a greater capacity than any previous Triumph twin cylinder unit, it produced only fractionally more horsepower than the 650cc but had considerably increased torque in its intermediate power range.

Claims for developed bhp no longer appeared in the catalogue, thereby eliminating once and for all the anomaly that had existed for years between the sizes of 'English' and 'American' horses! The answer to the inevitable horsepower question became like that of Rolls-Royce – enough!' But the increase in 'punch' demanded a triplex primary chain and a larger gearbox final drive sprocket.

The frame (now at series C) introduced for the T140 750cc models was lowered still further to a claimed 31 inch seat height thereby returning at long last to the previously acceptable pre-Umberslade dimensions.

In the Autumn of 1972 whilst the survivors of the Umberslade design team were digesting the failures encountered (with no cash available to implement the necessary changes to production design) the Chairman of Manganese Bronze Limited, Dennis Poore, also the Chairman of Norton Villiers Limited, had been invited by the Department of Trade and Industry to discuss with the Industrial Development Unit the total implications of Lord Shawcross's notification to them that BSA would shortly be unable to meet its obligation and that unless financial assistance was quickly forthcoming, Barclays Bank Limited would be called upon to appoint a receiver. Under closely guarded Department of Trade and Industry liaison, private discussions took place between BSA, Barclays Bank and Manganese Bronze in an attempt to determine a possible course to avert the impending disaster by utilising Norton Villiers, know-how in conjunction with limited Government financial support.

A solution appeared to be possible as, on 15th March 1973, the then Minister of State, Christopher Chataway, announced in Parliament that the Government had accepted the proposals to form a new company, bringing together the resources of Norton Villiers and BSA/Triumph in an attempt to save the British motorcycle industry.

Much has been written on the merits and virtues of closing a non-viable factory in favour of the operation of the smaller viable unit, or the alternative of terminating the latter to ensure the survival of the former, and then to operate the former more economically than before. BSA itself had previously initiated at least two independent investigations and reports into the Small Heath/Meriden question, and received both alternative solutions recommended. (Of course, the employees at both of the two factories knew only too well the solution that would most affect themselves).

Mr. Poore chose to retain Small Heath and to continue to operate the Norton Villiers plant at Wolverhampton, thereby deciding not to close Small Heath and to transfer all production to Meriden.

The press announced on 19th March 1973 that a new company called Norton Villiers Triumph Ltd (NVT) would be formed and the Department of Trade and Industry had conditionally agreed to provide £5 million of financial support. On 7th June an 'offer document' was sent to all BSA shareholders notifying them that Manganese Bronze had agreed to take up a half portion of the equity of the new company and if BSA Board's recommendation to the shareholders were now accepted then BSA would purchase the other half of the equity shareholding.

By 17th July, with £4.8 million injected by the DTI and with legal formalities completed, NVT became a reality and the Bonnie continued to be manufactured at Meriden. So it was with tremendous relief and eager anticipation that the Triumph factory at Meriden closed for the annual two weeks holiday. Why shouldn't there have been eager anticipation? All was to be well, with a promising future ahead of them, with a man at the helm who was known to all to have raised at least one well-known motorcycle facotry to commercial success from the ashes of bankruptcy. At least, that is what the men thought on that Friday evening when they left for their holidays.

However, the *Sunday Times* had made their opinion clear in their June 10th issue that they did not regard the reorganisation as doing any more than creating a breathing space and that the 'new industry' had only enough cash to make what it could from the current generation of superbikes for a further three years.

The Offer was Accepted! BSA shareholders received this offer document inviting them to transfer their stockholding to the proposed new company, NVT Limited, with a recommendation from the Board of BSA that the offer should be accepted. Thus, on the 17th July 1973, NVT became a reality

In August 1973 the annual works holidays were at an end, the scheduled production of 1973 models had been somehow completed, and the 1974 season's production was imminent. Edward Turner had died in retirement on 15th August, and the old BSA empire had fragmented and was now in ruins. Dennis Poore was now in control of the new parent company, NVT Limited. At that time, NVT Ltd owned NVT Manufacturing Limited at Armoury Road, Small Heath, Birmingham (the old BSA works) which had also been chosen as administrative headquarters, and NVT Manufacturing Ltd, Wolverhampton (the old Norton Villiers works) which was to continue production of the Norton motorcycle and also Meriden works, which retained its former name of Triumph Engineering Company Limited, at which production of the 1974 Bonnie was scheduled to continue.

Both the Triumph and Norton ranges of Motorcycles were to be distributed in the UK by a new company NT. Europe based at Andover in Hampshire and distributed overseas by Norton Triumph International which, from November 1973, was to be based at the former BSA Industrial Research Centre, located at Kitts Green, Birmingham.

Final design responsibility for Meriden products was to be that of Triumph's former Managing Director H. (Bert) Hopwood, but within a month of this announcement those at Meriden began to look concerned, maybe with justification.

Norton Triumph International, now at Kitts Green, had been chosen to house the new design team, the personnel for which were to be drawn from Small Heath (BSA) and Meriden (Triumph) led by Bert Hopwood (who had plans to build a 'V' five-cylinder machine) but who instead now decided to resign.

The August return to work at Meriden was marred by an industrial dispute, the result of a pre-holiday pay problem which was not resolved by the new NVT management until the end of the month. When settlement of the dispute was reached, the Meriden shop stewards, in an effort to cement relationships with the new administration, requested a meeting with Dennis Poore. (None of them had seen him at Meriden throughout the previous months of negotiation, which had obviously taken place).

In response to this request, a meeting was arranged for Friday, 14th September, to be held in the works canteen. The meeting was timed for midday, those present from the factory being members of the supervisory staff and trades union representatives. No one knows how, but rumours began to pass round the workshops whilst the meeting was in progress to the effect that Meriden was to be closed down. These rumours were being laughed off as ridiculous and stupid, until lunch time arrived and the workers at the factory were surprised to see newspaper sellers at the factory gates, selling the midday editions of the Local evening paper, the *Coventry Evening Telegraph* with the announcement in the Stop Press columns which confirmed the rumours. Dennis Poore was to close the Meriden works!

The closing date envisaged was to be February 1st 1974. This was the death knell of the Bonnie, born in 1959, and to be terminated in 1974 at the age of 15.

The 1,700 employees were at first bewildered, then very angry. Angry at the continued turmoil over the past three years that had created incessant and protracted delays on the production line. Angry at the complete lack of cohesion between Umberslade and the Meriden factory. Bitter at the gradual but continuous erosion of the personalised links between their own Triumph Sales Department (which had been moved to Small Heath some time previously) and the Meriden Production Planning Department, which had caused so many problems as the whole organisation had become more and more top heavy, remote and divisionalised.

So it was that an intensely close-linked factory, once proud of contributing fiercely to its own success and destiny and being individually aware of what it was doing and where it was going, had apparently been denied the flow of capital investment and forward planning activity, the consequence of which was that it was now forced to conclude that it had now been left to fend for itself.

Nevertheless, it does seem surprising that they came to the decision to close the factory down in view of the facts.

So it was quite understandable that the workers on the site were absolutely shattered when, fully aware of the continual failure to maintain the supply of materials, together with other disasters over the previous three years, they read in the local Coventry newspaper on the 15th September that Dennis Poore had given the reason for closure as being 'the Meriden factory having consistently fallen short of requirements, not because of any action of the workpeople, but because management had been unable to organise an adequate flow of supplies.'

All this, plus the fact that Christopher Chataway was reported to have given undertakings that the Meriden plant would remain open (*Coventry Evening Telegraph,* 15th September 1973) as one of the bases of parliamentary approval of the agreement, merely hardened the workers' attitude and strengthened their determination to do something about it.

It must be mentioned here that prior to the meeting with Dennis Poore on 14th September, the Meriden workers, having suffered the experiences of 1971/72/73 which had proved an almost total impediment to producing a worthwhile day's work, were eagerly awaiting Mr Poore's intervention, almost as the phoenix itself, to create a new epoch of success and stability. Obviously, they felt they knew far more intimately the circumstances surrounding their problems than they believed Mr Poore ever could. Hence the request for the meeting of the 14th September.

The evening edition of the *Coventry Evening Telegraph* on that 14th September 1973 carried headlines like 'we will fight – shop steward', and went on to quote 'even the Press knew of the intended closure before we did', or 'the management's excuse that work is not being turned out here won't hold water – it is because we have not had the components', and finally and simply 'the workers say the factory will not close'.

That night the Meriden factory was taken over by the workers and blockaded. The long sit-in had started.

No further Bonnies were to be made at Meriden for a long, long time.

TRIUMPH RULES UK !

RIDE A LIVING LEGEND
TRIUMPH

THE BLOCKADE AND BEYOND

At this point, the reader may well ask what this and subsequent events had to do with the Bonneville?

The total Meriden workforce had risen and rebelled as a man against the announcement to close the plant and the transfer of the product to some other place. At that time, they saw such plans as a total injustice and sought, by the toughest course of action known to them, a means whereby they could attempt to reverse that decision, although the action they took was itself an illegal act. The forcible takeover of the factory was complete, supported by a well organised picket programme on a shift rota system which, in the event, was to last for nearly 18 months. Communications were maintained to chain and block the gates. Nevertheless, and indicating the loyalty to the brand name Triumph, a number of the service staff had volunteered and agreed to relocate at the NVT organisation at Kitts Green in order to continue to maintain the Triumph service function to the outside world. At the same time limited initial consultation had already taken place with Christopher Chataway at the Department of Trade and Industry towards setting up some form of provisional agreement allowing the formation of a workers' co-operative. Following shortly afterwards, in December, the Triumph development department had also withdrawn from Meriden and was being set up again under Doug Hele, also at Kitts Green, when it was finally confirmed that any hope of Conservative Government financial backing for the co-operative was to prove totally unfounded. In consequence the possibility of any further dealings between the Meriden men and NVT fell through.

February 28th 1974 saw a general election, this time with a Labour Government ensuing which, predictably, resulted in Anthony Wedgwood Benn and Eric Heffer being placed in the industrial driving seat.

In March NVT sought to issue a writ to a Judge in Chambers to recover their rightful property, their factory, motorcycle stock, designs, jigs, tools and fixtures and material in progress at Meriden, which rapidly resulted in Wedgwood Benn's negotiations to avoid the possibility of any legal action taking place and to negotiate the initial movement of goods out of Meriden into the hands of NVT. At the same time Geoffrey Robinson, at that time head of Jaguar Cars (and later to become MP for Coventry North), also became involved in the overall negotiations which stretched as high and as far as Cabinet level.

Although by June that year (1974) the Triumph Trident three-cylinder machine had commenced rolling off the production line at Small Heath, the workers there remained unconvinced that the formation of a co-operative at Meriden was in their own long term interests, although following a June meeting at the Houses of Parliament with the minister, it had been agreed that the formation of a co-operative with Government backing was possible. Meriden plans would then have been to make 500 bikes a week with 879 employees.

The Lord Mayor of Coventry had already held a Civic Celebratory dinner in August 1974, although negotiations had not even yet been concluded. Of course the political climate in the country was such at that time that a second general election was held on 10th October before any further serious legal work could be undertaken. Nevertheless, after 13 months of negotiations a preliminary form of agreement had been reached and the stock of held motorcycles were gradually being moved out of Meriden (through the blockaded gates) for sale through the NVT distribution networks.

Life for the ex-employees at Meriden (redundancy notices had been served in November 1974) now became harder as a result of the failure of NVT to find an acceptable solution by procuring further Government financial support for their other two NVT factories at Small Heath and Wolverhampton, and with a reported 1200 employees who were involved at these two plants at the time, NVT would not finalise any arrangements to proceed with the Meriden Co-operative Agreement. In view of this impasse, Meriden therefore reinstated the blockade in full once again.

NVT were by now claiming a trading loss of £3½ million with a trading deficit of £5¾ million due, it was said, to their inability to utilise the Meriden facility, or alternatively, to be able to persuade the Government to finance a three-factory plan. Thus the workers outside Meriden steadfastly refused to accede to any suggestion of financial support to create a Meriden Co-operative until NVT had received equal assurances to those required for Meriden.

However, following a visit by Wedgwood Benn to Small Heath and Wolverhampton in November 1974, the Birmingham shop stewards finally agreed on 30th June 1975 to vote the co-op proposal as acceptable on the basis that the Government (once having set up the Meriden Co-operative) would support NVT in its scheme to proceed with a two-factory plan.

Production of the Bonnie had therefore recommenced at Meriden in February in anticipation of finalisation of the agreement and on 6th March 1975 the blockade finally ended. The Meriden Co-operative actually started operations – under the umbrella title of Synova Motors Limited, later to become Meriden Motorcycles Limited. NVT was paid the agreed sum of £3.9 million from a Government loan to the co-operative of £4.8 million and the Meriden Sales/Purchase Agreement became effective until July 1977. The Bonnie was again released to be set rolling, all the necessary factory tooling etc., in the meantime, having been kept well maintained, oiled and greased in anticipation of the great day. NVT was to be the sole customer and distribute all their products.

By 9th April the first wholly Co-operative built machine was ready for delivery (completion of the previous work-in-progress had occupied the initial re-start period) and on 25th June they had completed the last 750cc right-hand footshift model to be made at Meriden. In the intervening period, US legislation had dictated a changeover requiring left-hand gear change pedal operation. Sufficient work had been undertaken behind closed doors during the blockade to allow production of the new variant almost immediately, and the first machines were ready for delivery on 10th July 1975.

An announcement was made on 1st August 1975 that the Government had withdrawn a £4.0 million Exports Credit Guarantee Department Facility from NVT and at the same time, also confirmed the Cabinet refusal of any further financial support for the company. This proved to be the death knell for NVT Engineering at Wolverhampton, the old Norton Villiers factory which, during August 1975, was consequently wound up and placed in the hands of a liquidator. Considerable contraction immediately took place at Small Heath and Kitts Green (also during August), the old BSA plant ultimately having to be closed after completing a further 1,500 Trident models.

A receiver was then appointed for NVT Engineering Ltd at Small Heath on 20th October, followed by the appointment of the receiver for NVT International on 7th June 1976.

Thus NVT, after much re-forming and re-aligning both in the UK and USA, continued to handle the marketing and sale of the Meriden Co-operative Bonneville model. By the beginning of February 1976 production of the Bonnie had been happily continued at full steam whilst NVT had been unable to collect, ship and distribute. With such an impasse and over 3,000 motorcycles by this time in Meriden's inventory, creating a critical cash flow situation, the members of the co-operative agreed to an unprecedented stop and laid themselves off work for the subsequent five weeks to allow a full scale sorting out programme to be developed. The outcome was that GEC invested £1 million for 2,000 motorcycles, thereby injecting cash into the Meriden system and allowing a breathing space for the machines to be sold and the manufacturing process to be started up yet again.

Dennis Poore had already signified by this time that he wanted to withdraw from any future Triumph involvement and thus with further protracted and complicated negotiations, on the 2nd May 1977, assigned the marketing rights and assets to the Meriden company.

Meriden was free, Triumph were free, to design, develop, manufacture, market and distribute its own products once again after over 20 years of responsibility to another parent company. The feeling amongst the members was heady, but most realised it would be a long, hard uphill struggle to true freedom, born not only of financial and ideological concepts, but would also require sheer realistic commercial judgment. The Bonnie had been the underlying reason for that struggle, the driving force, the common bond. It should carry them into the future, far beyond the Bonneville model.

They deserve to succeed, I am sure they will. . . .

PART TWO

The Bonnie Year-by-Year
model description

The first Series 1959 Bonneville 120 for the home and general export markets. The frame was of single downtube construction, the forks incorporating the current instrument nacelle. Black oil tank and battery box assembly were specified with a two-level twinseat with its black vinyl top and side and white piping, deep valanced mudguards in Pearl Grey finish with Tangerine central stripes, Gold separating line, and with petrol tank in Pearl Grey (top half) with Tangerine lower half, and Gold separating lines

1959 model: Triumph T120 Bonneville

Technical Data

Engine

Bore:	71 mm (2.79 in)
Stroke:	82 mm (3.23 in)
Cylinder capacity:	649 cc (40 cu in)
Compression ratio:	8.5 : 1
Tappet clearance (cold): Inlet	0.002 in (0.10 mm)
Exhaust:	0.004 in (0.05 mm)
Valve timing:	34° BTC
	55° ABC
	48° BBC
	27° ATC
Ignition type:	Magneto
Ignition setting (fully advanced):	7/16 in (11 mm) 39° BTC
Bhp at rpm:	46 @ 6,500

Gearbox

		Internal
	Overall	Gearbox
Gear ratios:	Top: 4.57	1.0
	Third: 5.45	1.19
	Second: 7.75	1.69
	First: 11.20	2.44
Engine rpm/10 mph in top gear:	594	
Engine sprocket:	24 teeth	

Clutch sprocket:	43 teeth
Gearbox sprocket:	18 teeth
Rear wheel sprocket:	46 teeth
Front tyre size:	3.25 x 19 in (Ribbed)
Rear tyre size:	3.50 x 19 in (Universal)
Rear tyre revolutions per mile:	780

Frame

Petrol tank capacity:	4 Imp gallons (18 litres)
Oil tank capacity:	5 Imp pints (3 litres)
Wheel base:	55.75 in (142 cms)
Ground clearance:	5 in (12.7 cms)
Width over handlebars:	28.5 in (72.4 cms)
Weight:	404 lb (182 Kg)

Brakes

Front: Drum:	8 in dia single leading shoe
Rear: Drum:	7 in dia single leading shoe

Carburetters

Mixing chambers:	Amal Type 376/204
Float bowl:	Remote. Amal 14/617 – rubber mounted
Main jet:	240
Pilot jet:	25
Slide:	376/3½
Needle:	Type 'C' (3rd position)
Needle jet:	0.1065

Electrics

Lucas dynamo:	(Type E3L) 6 volt (A.V.C.) 60 watt
Lucas magneto:	Manual advance
Battery:	6 volt. 12 ampere hour

Colour

Pearl grey and Tangerine at the commencement of the 1959 season. The Tangerine was changed to Royal blue midway through the season, and the battery box and oil tank finished in Pearl grey.

1959 model: Pre-unit construction T120 model Bonneville 120
Commencing engine No. 020076

Engine unit

The 650cc ohv vertical twin engine unit was not until 1963 an integral unit with its gearbox and primary transmission. As a separate but complete power unit, it incorporated twin gear driven camshafts (E3134 inlet and E3325 exhaust), a cast iron cylinder barrel (plus 0.001 in diameter cylinder bores) with 1¹⁄₁₆ in diameter splayed inlet port alloy cylinder head. 8.5 : 1 compression ratio pistons (E3610) were specified which incorporated increased crown thickness at engine No. 021505, increased yet further by die replacement at engine No. 024242 with twin 1¹⁄₁₆ in diameter choke Amal Monobloc carburetter mixing chambers, and a single rubber mounted remote Amal GP float bowl, type 14/617. A new type one-piece forged EN.16B crankshaft with straight-sided cheeks was introduced with this model incorporating a bolt-on central cast iron flywheel. 'H' section RR56 alloy connecting rods were used incorporating plain big-ends, and shell bearing inserts. Dry sump lubrication was maintained by a plunger type pump, and the feed controlled by an oil pressure release valve and indicator. A gear driven dynamo and a magneto with manual advance mechanism were fitted.

Illustrating the centrally rubber mounted carburetter float bowl arrangement on the 1959 series Bonneville. This particular model had a Lucas K2FC 'Red Label' competition magneto, the timing cover patent plate still bearing the legend "T110."

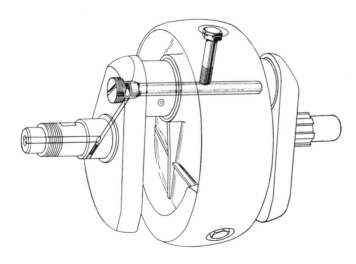

Straight sided crankshaft and flywheel assembly (finally in 3-versions) providing 50/70% and 85% balance factors. The 85% was to remain the standard for the T120 model up to the introduction of the T140

Gearbox
The gearbox was of Triumph design and manufacture utilising standard road ratio shafts and gears of hardened nickel and nickel chrome steel. Operation was through a positive stop right-hand side four-speed foot change mechanism. The gearbox camplate periphery was induction hardened from engine No. 023941.

Primary Transmission
A multi-plate clutch with Langite friction linings and rubber buffer shock absorber was attached to the gearbox mainshaft. Primary drive was housed in a polished aluminium oil bath primary chaincase, incorporating fill and level plugs. A simple primary chain/gearbox adjustment was provided with the primary drive acting through a 24 tooth engine sprocket. Longer screws were used to secure the outer primary cover to the inner at engine No. 022861 and an additional gearbox adjuster was fitted at 023111. The clutch sprocket centre bore was induction hardened at engine No. 024029.

Frame
The frame was of a brazed cradle type single front downtube design incorporating swinging arm rear suspension. 'Easy-lift' centre stand and optional prop stand were fitted and provision was made for fitment of an anti-theft lock in the steering head.

Rear Suspension Units
Girling hydraulically damped (100 lb/in rate springs), adjustable for varying loads, with chromed lower dirt shield.

Forks
The Triumph design telescopic pattern forks incorporated internal oil damping and were fitted with a manual steering damper. The front wheel stand was also specified as standard.

Fuel Tank
All-welded steel tank with quick release filler cap. A chrome-plated parcel grid was fitted as standard.

Oil Tank
The oil tank incorporated an anti-froth tower in a one-piece unit with the air cleaner, battery and tool kit container.

Instrument Nacelle
The headlamp nacelle of Triumph patented design on top of the forks enclosed the headlamp and incorporated instruments, cut-out and switch gear in the top panel. The instruments were internally illuminated.

Brakes
Front:	Full width hub, heavily finned, 8 in diameter single leading shoe drum brake.
Rear:	7 in diameter with cast iron drum integral with a ·46 tooth rear chain sprocket.

Wheels
Triumph designed front and rear wheels with plated spokes and rims.

Mudguards
Deep valanced front and rear mudguard, with rear lifting handle. The front mudguard was spot welded to the centre mounting bridge to obviate cracking at engine No. 021941.

Exhaust System
A 1½ in bore internal diameter exhaust system was fitted, originally with E3816/7 straight-through T110 silencers, later replaced by E3651/2 at engine No. 024337.

Air Filter
Air cleaner equipment not specified.

Electrical Equipment
Electrical generation was by Lucas 6 volt 60 watt dynamo E3L-L10 feeding a 12 ampere/hour 6 volt battery. The headlamp was fitted with a 30/34 watt pre-focused bulb, beam adjustment achieved by means of an adjustable rim. A combined stop/tail lamp was fitted. A much more robust voltage regulator (Lucas 37725H) was fitted from engine No. 024137.

Speedometer
Smiths 120 mph (180 kph) chronometric type with multi-rpm scale, internal illumination, odometer and trip recorder was fitted into the nacelle top cover.

Handlebars
Home or Overseas specification fitted with a quick-action twist-grip which incorporated an adjustable friction control. The handlebar featured an integral horn push and ball-ended clutch and brake levers with built-in cable adjusters were fitted. A mid-season specification change resulted in straighter sporty type U.K. handlebars being fitted to the U.K. and general export models.

Twinseat
Of Triumph design, the first models had a two-level twinseat with black top, white piping, black sides and no lower rim trim band. Later models in the 1959 season had the narrow sports type with latex foam cushion. The cover then had a black waterproof vynide top and sides with white piping and grey lower rim trim band.

Late 1959 Bonneville 120, home model, fitted with single level sports type twinseat, black vinyl top, white piping, black sides and grey lower rim trim band, fuel tank Pearl Grey top half, Azure Blue lower half, Gold lines and Pearl Grey oil tank and battery box assembly

Finish

Frame:	Black
Forks:	Black, including the nacelle and instrument panel.
Mudguards:	Pearl grey, Tangerine centre strip with gold lining
Fuel tank:	Two-tone Pearl grey top/Tangerine lower half with gold separating lines
Oil tank:	Black
Battery box:	Black

Later 1959 models were affected by the mid-season change to Pearl grey and Royal blue. The oil tank and battery box were amended to Pearl grey.

Extras
Quickly detachable rear wheel, pillion footrests, prop stand and steering lock were available as extra equipment.

US model east coast variant – two-level black vinyl twinseat, white piping, fuel tank Pearl Grey top half, Azure Blue lower half, with Gold separating lines. Pearl Grey mudguards with Azure Blue centre stripe and Gold separating lines, with Pearl Grey oil tank and battery box assembly

U.S. Alternatives

Magneto:	Lucas K2FC (Red label) manual
Fuel tank:	3 gallon (Imp)
Handlebars:	Overseas (Flanders) pattern complete with all the necessary increased length control cables
Twinseat:	East Coast – Two-level – all black finish
	West Coast – Narrow type seat, with safety strap – all black finish
Finish:	As U.K. models. Two-tone Pearl grey/Tangerine paint finish changed in mid-season to Pearl grey/Royal blue, with oil tank and battery/tool box finished in Pearl grey.

1960 model, home and general export. The instrument nacelle was dropped in favour of a more sporty look utilising a chromed headlamp and front fork gaiters. A new Duplex frame was specified with the carburetter float bowl suspended by a threaded rod through the metalastik rubber bush mounted in the engine cylinder head torque steady plate. The two-level twinseat returned, incorporating a black lower rim trim band

1960 model: Pre-unit construction T120 model Bonneville 120
Commencing engine No. 029424, and D.101 onwards

Engine Unit
A 650cc ohv vertical twin with two gear driven camshafts (E3134 inlet E3325 exhaust) incorporating a cast iron cylinder barrel (plus 0.001 in diameter) with 1¹⁄₁₆ in diameter splayed inlet port alloy cylinder head, 8.5 : 1 compression ratio pistons, twin 1¹⁄₁₆ in diameter choke Amal Monobloc carburetter mixing chambers with rubber bush/rod suspended remote Amal float bowl type 14/624. The one-piece forged EN.16B crankshaft with straight-sided cheeks and radial (3) bolt-on central cast iron flywheel continued, incorporating the 'H' section RR.56 alloy connecting rods and plain big-end shell bearing inserts. Dry sump lubrication was achieved with a plunger type pump and the feed controlled by incorporating an oil pressure relief valve and indicator. A crankshaft mounted a.c. alternator with a gear driven Lucas K2F magneto incorporating an auto advance mechanism was fitted.

Gearbox
The gearbox was of Triumph design and manufacture incorporating standard road ratio shafts and gears made of hardened nickel and nickel chrome steel. Control was via a positive stop four-speed right-hand foot change.

Primary Transmission
The multi-plate clutch with Langite friction linings and rubber buffer shock absorber was mounted on the gearbox mainshaft and incorporated in the separate polished aluminium oil bath with fill and level plugs. Primary drive was through a 22 teeth engine drive sprocket.

Illustrating the method of assembly of the centrally suspended rubber bush and rod mounted remote float chamber on the 1960 model

Frame
A new brazed cradle duplex twin downtube front frame with rear swinging arm suspension was introduced, the easy-lift centre stand and optional prop stand continued for 1960 as did the provision for an anti-theft steering head lock.

Forks
A new Triumph design telescopic pattern fork with fork gaiters and internal two-way damping was introduced. Fitted with manual steering damper equipment.

Fuel Tank
The all-welded steel tank, 3-point rubber mounted, located and retained in situ with a central rubber lined plated strap. A quick release filler cap and chrome-plated parcel grid were fitted as standard equipment.

Oil Tank
The oil tank incorporated an anti-froth tower in conjunction with a one-piece unit complete with air cleaner, battery and tool kit container.

Brakes

Front:	Full width hub, heavily finned with 8 in diameter single leading shoe drum brake.
Rear:	7 in diameter with cast iron drum integral with 43 teeth rear chain sprockets.

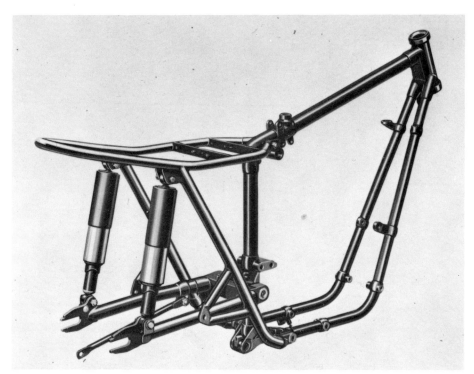

The Bonnie duplex frame for 1960, subsequently to be re-inforced with the addition of a lower tank rail for the following season

Wheels
Triumph designed front and rear wheels with plated spokes and rims were fitted.

Mudguards
A new sports type front mudguard and steel sports rear mudguard were now fitted.

Exhaust System
The 1½ in diameter exhaust pipes were fitted in conjunction with a muted silencer system.

Air Filter
Air cleaner equipment not specified.

Electrical Equipment
Lucas 6 volt a.c. generator system, rectified to d.c. fed the 12 ampere/hour 6 volt battery via a rectifier and ammeter in the detachable chromed headlamp, with 30/24 watt pre-focus bulb. A combined stop/tail lamp was fitted. The lighting switch was now located on the right side of the machine immediately below the twinseat nose.

Speedometer
Smiths 140 mph (240 kph) chronometric type with multi-rpm scale, internal illumination, odometer and trip recorder was fitted.

Handlebars
The chrome-plated Home and Overseas (Flanders) specification with a quick action twist-grip incorporating adjustable friction control and integral horn bulb was specified. A cut-out button, clutch and brake ball-ended levers with built-in cable adjusters were specified.

The US Variant of the 1960 T120, the T120R model

Twinseat
Of Triumph design with latex foam cushion. Black waterproof vynide cover with white piping and black lower rim trim band were now specified. Twinseat bolted in situ, and not hinged.

Finish

Frame:	Black
Forks:	Black
Mudguards:	Front: Pearl grey, Azure blue centre stripe, gold lined
	Rear: Pearl grey, Azure blue centre stripe, gold lined
Fuel tank:	Two-toned Pearl grey top/Azure blue lower half, gold separating line
Oil tank:	Pearl grey
Battery box:	Pearl grey

Extras
Quickly detachable rear wheel (43 teeth), pillion footrests, prop stand and steering lock.

U.S. Alternatives

Magneto:	Lucas K2FC (Red label) auto
Fuel tank:	3 gallon (Imp)
Handlebars:	Overseas pattern complete with all the necessary longer control cables.
Twinseat:	Safety strap fitted to West Coast models as standard equipment.
Exhaust System:	High level exhaust pipes and silencers were fitted to U.S. Competition models.
Finish:	As U.K.

A 1960 USA T120'C' Competition model, illustrating the new duplex front frame being given the obvious seal of approval by John Surtees

The 1961 T120 Bonneville model discontinued the specification of the remote carburetter float bowl and fitted twin standard Amal monobloc carburetters. The colour finish was Silver and Sky-Blue lined in Gold.

1961 model: Pre-unit construction T120 model Bonneville 120
Commencing engine No. D7727

Engine Unit

Continuing as a separate 650cc ohv vertical twin unit with twin gear driven camshaft E.3134 inlet and E3325 exhaust. The cast iron cylinder barrel (plus 0.001 in bore diameter) 8.5 : 1 compression ratio pistons and 1¹⁄₁₆ in diameter splayed inlet port alloy cylinder head, fitting twin 1¹⁄₁₆ in diameter choke Amal Monobloc integral float bowl carburetters. The one-piece forged EN.16B crankshaft with straight-sided cheeks, and radial (three) bolt-on central cast iron flywheel, 'H' section RR.56 alloy connecting rods with plain big-end shell bearing inserts continued. Dry sump lubrication was maintained with a plunger type pump in conjunction with an oil pressure release valve and indicator. A crankshaft mounted a.c. alternator with a gear driven Lucas K2F magneto incorporating an auto advance mechanism was fitted.

Gearbox

A Triumph designed and manufactured gearbox incorporating standard road ratio shafts and gears of hardened nickel and nickel-chromed steel was fitted. This year needle roller layshaft and needle roller layshaft bearings were fitted. Control was effected by a positive stop four-speed right-hand foot change. Dual primary chain-gearbox adjusters were incorporated for 1961 models.

Primary Transmission

The multi-plate clutch with improved Langite non-stick friction linings and rubber buffer shock absorber incorporated in the polished aluminium oil bath with filler and level plugs. The primary drive engine sprocket was reduced by one tooth to 21 teeth.

The 1961/2 Bonnie duplex frame incorporating the lower tank rail

Frame

The brazed duplex cradle type twin front downtube front frame with revised head angle, and an extra reinforcing lower tank rail, continued with the earlier rear frame section and swinging arm rear suspension. Easy-lift centre stand and optional prop stand continued together with the provision for anti-theft steering head lock.

Rear Suspension Units

Girling hydraulically damped (100 lb/in rate springs) adjustable for varying loads were fitted.

Forks

The Triumph designed telescopic forks with internal progressive two-way damping continued but now incorporated aluminium spacer sleeves. Fitted with manual steering damper.

Fuel Tank

A new 3 (Imp) gallon all-welded steel fuel tank with reinforced nose bridge piece, with front mounting feet providing a 3-point rubber mounting, was located and retained by a central rubber-lined chrome-plated strap. Quick release filler cap. Petrol taps were now treated with P.T.F.E. film. The chrome-plated parcel grid continued to be fitted as standard.

Oil Tank

A new oil tank with revised anti-vibration mountings, and incorporating an anti-froth tower in a one-piece unit complete with air cleaner, battery and tool kit container.

Brakes

Front:	Full width hub, heavily finned with 8 in diameter single leading shoe drum brake.
Rear:	7 in diameter with cast iron drum integral with 43 teeth rear chain sprocket.

Fully floating brake shoes front and rear brakes.

The 1961 fully-floating front brake shoe arrangement fitted standard until the 1966 season

Wheels

Triumph designed front and rear wheels with plated spokes and rims were fitted.

Mudguards

Sports type painted mudguards were fitted front and rear.

Exhaust System

1½ in internal diameter exhaust pipes and muted silencer system was fitted.

Air Filters

Air cleaner equipment not specified or fitted.

Electrical Equipment

Lucas 6 volt a.c. generator system, rectified to d.c., feeding the 12 ampere/hour 6 volt battery via a rectifier and ammeter in the detachable chrome headlamp fitted with 30/24 watt pre-focus bulb. A combined stop/tail light was fitted. The lighting switch was located on the right side of the machine below the twinseat nose.

Speedometer

Smiths 120 mph (180 kph) chronometric type with multi-rpm scale, internal illumination, odometer and trip recorder.

Handlebars

The chrome-plated Home and Overseas (Flanders) specification with quick-action twist-grip incorporating adjustable friction control and integral horn push was fitted. The cut-out button, ball-ended clutch and brake levers with built-in cable adjusters were fitted.

Twinseat

Of Triumph design with latex foam cushion covered in black waterproof vynide with white piping and black lower rim trim band. The twinseat was bolted in situ and not hinged.

Finish

Frame:	Black
Forks:	Black
Mudguards:	Front: Silver with Sky blue centre stripe, gold lined
	Rear: Silver with Sky blue centre stripe, gold lined
Petrol tank:	Two-tone, Sky blue top, silver lower half, gold separating line
Oil tank:	Silver
Battery box:	Silver

Extras

Quickly detachable rear wheel (43 teeth), pillion footrest, prop stand, and steering lock.

U.S. Alternatives

Magneto:	Lucas K2FC (Red label) auto
Handlebars:	Overseas pattern complete with all necessary extended control cables.
Twinseat:	Safety strap fitted to West Coast models as standard equipment.
Finish:	As U.K. models

The U.S. models were now supplied in two basic variants:

'R' – Road models – with Universal rear and ribbed front tyre.

'C' – Competition models – with Trials Universal tyres, upswept exhaust system, crankcase undershield and competition (Wader) magneto.

View of the right-hand side of the 1961 US east coast T120C competition model with upswept exhaust pipes, leg shields and crankcase undershield

Left side of the same model, which in this particular photograph is fitted with a black battery box and oil tank assembly

1962 Export T120 with petrol tank finished with Flame top/Silver Sheen lower half (Gold separating lines), Silver Sheen guards, Flame centre stripe and Gold Separating lines. The home and standard export models were Sky Blue tank, top half, with Silver lower half, Gold separating lines, with Silver Sheen guards, Sky Blue centre stripe and Gold separating lines

1962 model: Pre-unit construction T120 model Bonneville 120
Commencing engine No. D.15789

Models: T120 T120R T120C

Engine Unit
The 650cc vertical twin separate engine unit was now fitted with two three keyway cam wheel pinions driving camshafts E3134 inlet and E3325 exhaust. The cast iron cylinder barrel (plus 0.001 in bore diameter) with 1¹⁄₁₆ in diameter splayed inlet port alloy cylinder head, 8.5 : 1 compression ratio pistons continued with 1¹⁄₁₆ in diameter choke Amal Monobloc carburetters. The one-piece forged EN.16B crankshaft fitted with a new bolt-on central flywheel providing 71% balance factor, was subsequently superseded by introducing the new pear-shaped crankshaft (E4493) providing 85% balance factor after engine No. D.17043. The 'H' section RR56 alloy con rods with plain big-end shell bearing inserts continued. Dry sump lubrication was maintained with a plunger type oil pump and the feed pressure was maintained with an integral release valve and indicator. The crankshaft mounted a.c. alternator continued as did the gear driven Lucas K2F magneto incorporating an auto advance mechanism.

Gearbox
The Triumph designed and manufactured standard road ratio gearbox with shafts and gears of hardened nickel and nickel chrome steel, now incorporating needle and roller layshaft bearings and positive stop four-speed right-hand foot change continued, together with the dual primary chain/gearbox adjusters.

Primary Transmission
A multi-plate clutch with Langite friction linings and rubber buffer shock absorber was fitted to the gearbox mainshaft and incorporated in the polished aluminium chaincase oil bath incorporating filler and level plugs.

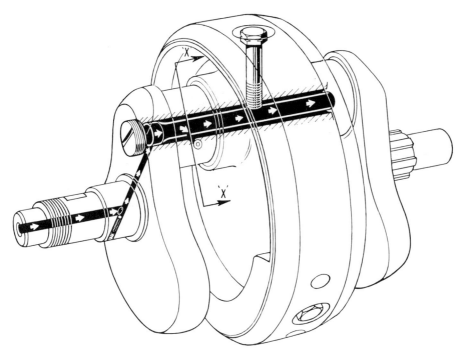

The heavy flywheel assembly replaced the 'narrow' version which was introduced earlier in 1966, retaining the 85% balance factor

Frame
A brazed cradle duplex type frame with twin front downtube front frame section and swinging arm rear suspension was specified. Easy-lift centre stand, and optional prop stand together with provision for anti-theft steering head lock continued.

Rear Suspension Units
Girling hydraulically damped (145 lb/in rate springs) adjustable for varying loads were fitted.

Forks
Triumph designed telescopic forks with internal springs and progressive two-way damping were fitted and a manual steering damper incorporated.

Fuel Tank
Three or four gallon (as required) all-welded steel fuel tank, 3 point rubber mounted and located and retained by a central rubber-lined plated strap. Fuel tank incorporating a quick release filler cap. Reserve fuel tap now specified. Chrome-plated parcel grid fitted as standard equipment.

Oil Tank
An oil tank with anti-vibration mounting, in a one-piece unit, with air cleaner, battery case and tool kit container was fitted.

Brakes
Front:	Full width hub, heavily finned with 8 in diameter single leading shoe drum brake.
Rear:	7 in diameter with cast iron drum integral with 43 teeth rear chain sprocket.

Fully floating shoes fitted to both front and rear brakes.

85

Wheels
Triumph designed wheels with plated spokes and rims were fitted.

Mudguards
Painted steel front and rear mudguards were specified.

Exhaust System
1½ in diameter exhaust pipes and muted silencer exhaust system.

Air Filter
No air cleaner equipment was specified as standard.

Electrical Equipment
Lucas 6 volt a.c. generator system, rectified to d.c. and feeding the 12 ampere/hour 6 volt battery via a silicone rectified, and 2AR ammeter in the (non-Q.D.) chromed headlamp, with 30/24 watt pre-focus bulb. A combined stop/tail light was fitted from D18419 onwards. Lucas 88S.A. switch was located on the right side of the machine immediately below the twinseat nose.

Speedometer
Smiths 140 mph (240 kph) chronometric type, with multi-rpm scale, internally illuminated odometer and trip recorder was used.

Handlebars
Chrome-plated Home and Overseas (Flanders) specification with quick-action twist-grip, incorporating friction control and integral horn push was used. Cut-out button clutch and brake controls incorporating ball-ended levers and built-in cable adjusters were fitted.

Twinseat
Of Triumph design with latex foam cushion, covered in waterproof vynide with grey top, white piping, black sidewalls, and grey lower rim trim band.

Finish

Frame:	Black
Forks:	Black
Mudguard:	Front – Silver, Sky blue centre stripe – gold lined
	Rear – Silver, Sky blue centre stripe – gold lined
Petrol tank:	Two-tone, Sky blue top, silver lower half, gold separating line
Oil tank:	Black
Battery box:	Black

Extras
A quickly detachable rear wheel (43 teeth), pillion footrest, prop stand and steering lock continued to be available.

U.S. Alternatives

Magneto:	Lucas K2FC (Red label) auto – 'R' models
	Lucas K2FC (Red label) Wader auto – 'C' models
Fuel Tank:	4 gallon (Imp) – 'R' models D.15794 onwards
	3 gallon (Imp) – 'C' models
Handlebars:	Overseas pattern complete with all the necessary extended control cables.
Twinseat:	Safety strap fitted to West Coast models as standard equipment.

1962 T120R model. The US model specified Flame/Silver paint finish as standard for this season

Alternator:	Low/low stator (47183) fitted
Finish:	Mudguard – Front – Silver Sheen, Flame stripe, gold lined
	Rear – Silver Sheen, Flame stripe, gold lined
	Petrol tank: Two-tone Flame top, Silver Sheen lower half, gold separating line
	Oil Tank: Silver
	Battery box: Silver

The 1963 Model T120. The first unit construction 650cc Triumph Bonneville 120 model in Alaskan White, Gold stripe and lined Black

1963 model: Unit construction T120 model Bonneville 120
Commencing engine No. DU.101

Models: T120 T120R T120C

Engine Unit

650cc vertical twin cylinder engine of unit construction integral with the primary drive and gearbox assemblies, with two (3 keyway) crankshaft, intermediate and camshaft (wider section) pinions driving the inlet camshaft (E4819 – E3134 form with breather tube) and exhaust camshaft (E4855 – E3325 form with contact breaker extension and tachometer drive).

A Nine Stud cast iron cylinder barrel was fitted in conjunction with the $1\frac{1}{16}$ in diameter splayed inlet port Nine Stud alloy cylinder head, the eight main cylinder head/rocker box holding-down bolt centres being increased diametrically outward to obviate any future possibility of cylinder head/valve seat cracking problems, and to allow for future anticipated increases in inlet port diameter. An additional $\frac{5}{16}$ in diameter central bolt was added to ensure an adequate gas seal between the cylinders.

8.5 : 1 compression ratio pistons, finned rocker boxes and rocker box caps coined to lock into externally fitted locking springs. A new crankshaft (E4643) was fitted incorporating an extended right-hand ground surface journal to accommodate the new timing side oil seal, in lieu of the previous timing cover phosphor bronze oil control bush, but continuing to utilise 'H' section RR56 polished connecting rods with plain big-end shell bearing inserts. Bolt-on central flywheel (using Loctite to secure the three fixing bolts – in lieu of the previous E2288 serrated lock washers) giving 85% balance factor. Dry sump lubrication with plunger type pump and oil pressure relief valve and indicator. Crankshaft mounted Lucas a.c. alternator rotor with exhaust camshaft driven (Lucas 4CA) twin contact breaker assembly neatly mounted in a timing cover.

Gearbox

Integral with the engine and primary transmission unit. Standard ratio shafts and gears of hardened nickel and nickel chrome steel were fitted, the needle roller layshaft bearings continuing in conjunction with a new layshaft incorporating a speedometer drive end to suit the new unit construction speedometer gearbox drive requirements within the revised gearbox inner cover. (A range of layshaft drive/driven pinions were made available to provide 1600 rpm, to suit various gearbox drive sprocket/rear wheel sprocket/tyre size combinations.) Positive stop, four-speed foot change was retained.

Primary Transmission

The new integral primary transmission unit comprised a new multi-plate clutch assembly housed in a new (58 teeth) cast iron clutch housing, with Langite cork friction linings, but incorporating an additional driving plate. Three heavy duty clutch springs and a three vane clutch shock absorber unit incorporating a bronze-faced clutch thrust washer to eliminate clutch rattle, provided a heavier duty clutch of increased resilience, operated by a new three-ball clutch operating mechanism in the gearbox outer cover.

The ⅜ in pitch duplex primary drive chain (29 teeth drive sprocket) ran in conjunction with a circulatory oil feed system to the inside of the chain, and externally adjustable chain tensioner. Accessible filler and level plugs were provided within the polished aluminium cover. In the rear wall of the primary cover an oiler tube and metering jet were incorporated to ensure adequate rear chain lubrication.

Frame

The brazed cradle type frame now incorporated a new single large diameter heavy section front downtube front frame, the lower frame section of which carried an entirely new rear suspension swinging arm lug, which itself was integrally mounted with a new rear engine plate, making the fore and aft axis of the machine extremely rigid, in conjunction with a stiffer rear swinging arm. Easy-lift centre stand, with provisions for an anti-theft steering head lock, engaging in the front fork slotted stem was standard equipment.

Forks.

Triumph designed telescopic forks with internal springs were fitted providing progressive two-way damping. A manual steering damper was specified.

Fuel Tank

Three or four (Imp) gallon (as required). All-steel welded tank, rubber mounted and bolted (x 2) front and (x 1) rear now specified with a quick release filler cap, reserve fuel tap, chrome-plated parcel grid, chromed centre styling strip, and stick-on knee grips.

Oil Tank

Bolted to two rubber mounted battery carried frame cross straps with a bolted lower fixing to the front frame swinging arm mounting lug.

Brakes

Front:	Full width 8 in diameter finned cast iron hub with single leading shoe drum brake.
Rear:	7 in diameter cast iron drum integral with (46 teeth) rear chain sprocket.

Fully floating shoes fitted on both front and rear brakes.

Wheels

Triumph designed 3.25 x 18 in front and 3.50 x 18 in rear wheels with plated spokes and rims.

Mudguards

Painted steel front and rear mudguards.

Exhaust System

1½ in diameter exhaust pipes and resonator silencer system fitted.

Air Filters

Separate 'pancake' type air filters available as an optional extra.

Electrical Equipment

Fitted with a Lucas 6 volt a.c. generator system, and feeding the MLZ9E 12 ampere/hour 6 volt battery via a silicone rectifier and 2 AR ammeter in the (non-Q.D.) chromed headlamp with 30/24 watt pre-focus bulb. The ignition was controlled by two Lucas MA6 ignition coils rubber mounted on the frame, beneath the fuel tank, in conjunction with the twin exhaust camshaft driven Lucas 4CA twin contact breaker unit and auto advance mechanism mounted in the timing cover. The charging circuit incorporated a 25 ampere fuse, whilst Lucas 88SA (multi-pin plug/socket) type lighting and ignition switches were installed (lighting switch uppermost) in a switch panel on the left side of the machine below the nose of the hinged twinseat. The ignition system featured an emergency (EMG) starting in the event of a flat battery. A combined stop/tail light was included in the electrical/lighting system.

Speedometer and Tachometer

Smiths 140 mph (1600 cable rpm calibration) chronometric type speedometer specified as standard equipment. Tachometer was not specified as standard, but the drive facility was provided by means of an externally mounted crankcase union adaptor and direct cable drive available from the exhaust camshaft when required.

Handlebars

⅞ in diameter chrome-plated Home and Overseas specification, anti-vibration rubber Metalastic bush mounted, in handlebar clamp bolts (with additional support rubbers for the high rise U.S. specification handlebars). Quick-action twist-grip incorporating friction control fitted and integral dipswitch and horn push (no cut-out button fitted on this model). Clutch and brake levers with built-in cable adjusters and ball-ended levers were specified as standard equipment.

USA east coast T120R model

USA west coast model T120R

Twinseat
Triumph designed, two-level cushion seat covered in waterproof vynide, grey top, white piping, with black sides and grey lower rim band.

Finish

Frame:	Black
Forks:	Black
Mudguard:	Front – Alaskan white, gold stripe, black lined
	Rear – Alaskan white, gold stripe, black lined

Petrol tank:	Alaskan white
Oil tank:	Black
Switch panel:	Black

Extras

Quickly detachable rear wheel (46 teeth) pillion footrests, prop stand and front fork steering lock available as extra equipment.

U.S. Alternatives

Handlebars:	Overseas pattern (including the necessary additional rubber and cup mounting washers, and longer control cables – twin rotor friction controlled twist-grip).
Wheels:	3.25 x 19 in front and 4.00 x 18 in rear were available as required.
Air filter:	Twin 'pancake' (coarse paper) type fitted as required.
Colours:	As U.K.

USA east coast version of the Competition Model T120C

High Performance Components

Piston:	8.5 : 1 compression ratio, crown machined to accept $\frac{3}{32}$ in increased diameter inlet and exhaust valves, together with increased depth D/24 compression and oil control rings.
Cylinder head:	1⅛ in diameter inlet ports and carburetter adaptors with valve seats to suit the 1$\frac{19}{32}$ in diameter inlet and 1$\frac{7}{16}$ in diameter Nimonic exhaust valves.
Main bearings:	Double lipped roller (E2879).

91

The USA west coast T120C model had seat safety strap to comply with legislative requirements, and a straight-through exhaust system as standard equipment

Camshaft: Copper plated inlet and exhaust (E3134 form) with E3059R (1⅛ in radius) cam followers (tappets).

Carburetters: 1⅛ in diameter choke Amal type 389 mixing chamber.

Float chamber (remote): Amal 14/624 flexibly mounted.

Close ratio gears: with special (1600 rpm) speedometer drive gear.

Clutch springs: Heavy duty (T1830).

Folding kick-starter lever: (T1869).

Rear-set footrests, brake pedal and rear engine plate.

Wheels: WM2 – 19 rims front and rear. MZ41 brake linings.

Racing handlebars: Rear lifting handles and front headlamp bracket for fixing racing number plates, complete with 'racing' front fork pinch bolts.

Tachometer: With combined speedometer/tachometer bracket. Tacho driven directly by cable and union adaptor from the left end of the exhaust camshaft (i.e 2 : 1 engine/tacho speed calibration).

1964 650cc T120 home and general export Bonneville 120 Model. Colours were Alaskan White and Gold, with the White mudguards, Gold centre stripe and Black lined

1964 model: Unit construction T120 model Bonneville 120
Commencing engine No. DU.5825

Models: T120 Bonneville 120 T120C Competition Sports Bonneville T120
T120R Speedmaster T120C T.T. Special

Engine Unit

650cc unit construction vertical twin cylinder, with inlet and exhaust camshafts, cast iron cylinder block with 1⅛ in diameter splayed inlet port alloy cylinder head, 8.5 : 1 compression ratio pistons, to accommodate 1¹⁹⁄₃₂ in diameter head inlet, and 1⁷⁄₁₆ in diameter head exhaust valves and two Amal 1⅛ in diameter choke Monobloc carburetters. The carburetter inlet port adaptors were fitted with an induction balance pipe. Finned rocker boxes with locking type rocker box caps were specified. A one-piece forged crankshaft with a bolt-on central flywheel, 'H' section RR56 polished alloy connecting rods with plain big-end shell bearing inserts assembled with 3-spot main bearings and fitted into a revised crankcase casting with revised internal configuration to improve the oil pump scavenge characteristic, at the same time incorporating a new sump filter and drain plug arrangement. Location of the breather disc in the inlet camshaft left bush housing improved internal crankcase depression, the external breather pipe now being connected to the new oil tank froth tower via a connector 'T' piece. Dry sump lubrication continued with a plunger type pump controlled by the oil pressure release valve incorporating an indicator button. The crankshaft incorporated the Lucas alternator rotor, with the exhaust camshaft driven Lucas 4CA twin contact breaker assembly mounted in the timing cover.

Gearbox

Integral with the engine unit, the standard ratio shafts and gears were of hardened nickel and nickel chrome steel. Needle roller bearings supported the layshaft. Revised gearbox sprocket/high gear larger splines were introduced on standard, close and wide ratio high gear sleeves, to ease current production problems. A kick-starter spindle oil seal was incorporated in the gearbox outer cover. Positive stop, four-speed foot change continued.

93

Primary Transmission

Multi-plate clutch with cork friction linings, improved clutch shock absorber rubbers, the clutch being actuated by a three-ball thrust mechanism in the gearbox outer cover. Renold ⅜ in pitch duplex primary chain drive with external tensioner adjustment and lubricated by a recirculating oil feed to the inside of the chain. Rear chain lubrication by means of a metering jet in the rear of the primary chaincase, which incorporated accessible filler and level plugs in the polished alloy cover.

Frame

Brazed cradle type with single downtube front frame and swinging arm rear suspension. The footrests were changed to mount directly onto the rear engine plates to provide increased ground clearance, at the same time allowing a re-routing of the rear brake rod to the inside of the left suspension unit, and redesign of the footbrake pedal.

A new type 'pull' stoplight switch was fitted further rearward, onto new deeper section rear chainguard. The easy-lift centre stand now had a brazed-in operating arm, replacing the previous cottered version, with provision for an anti-theft lock continuing in the frame steering headlock.

Forks

Triumph designed telescopic forks with external fork springs, the lower spring carrier equipped with double lipped oil seals, rubber fork gaiters and increased oil capacity two-way damping. Fitted with manual steering damper, now having a simple rubber bush added to the damper spindle to eliminate the annoying tendency to unwind in use.

Fuel Tank

Three or four (Imp) gallon, all-steel welded tank, rubber mounted and bolted front (x 2) and rear (x 1). Quick release filler cap, reserve fuel tap, chrome-plated parcel grid, chromed centre styling strip and stick-on knee grips continued from last year.

Oil Tank

Bolted at the top to the two rubber mounted battery carrier frame cross straps, with a new rubber insulated lower spigot mounting support. The engine breather connected by a 'T' piece connector to the oil tank anti-froth tower. Drain plug facility was now incorporated in the tank, and both oil feed and return pipes incorporated clips at both ends.

Rear Suspension Units

Girling hydraulically damped suspension units adjustable for varying loads were fitted.

Brakes

Front:	Full width 8 in diameter finned cast iron hub, with single leading shoe drum brake.
Rear:	7 in diameter cast iron drum integral with (46 teeth) rear chain sprocket.

Fully floating shoes were fitted on both front and rear brakes.

Wheels

Triumph designed 3.25 x 18 in ribbed front and 3.50 x 18 in Dunlop K70 Gold Seal rear wheels. Spokes and rims were plated.

Mudguards

Mudguards of painted steel front and rear with Competition type front mudguard mountings and front wheel stand on all models.

Exhaust System

1½ in diameter downswept exhaust pipes and non-resonator silencers specified.

Air Filter
An entirely new single unit air filter box was introduced, equipped with a replaceable paper element, feeding both carburetters and fitted to overseas models were specified.

Electrical Equipment
Lucas 6 volt a.c. generator system, rectified to d.c. feeding the MLZ9E 12 ampere/hour 6 volt battery via a silicon rectified and 2AR ammeter in the chromed headlamp, incorporating a 30/24 watt pre-focus bulb. Ignition controlled by two Lucas MA6 ignition coils rubber mounted onto the frame beneath the fuel tank and operated by the exhaust camshaft driven Lucas 4CA twin contact breaker and auto advance unit mounted in the timing cover housing. A 25 ampere fuse was incorporated in the charging circuit. Lucas 88SA (multi-pin plug/socket) type lighting and ignition switches were installed (lighting uppermost) in the switch panel on the left side of the machine beneath the nose of the hinged twinseat. EMG starting was available in the event of a discharged battery. A combined stop/tail rear light was fitted as standard.

Speedometer and Tachometer
New type Smiths magnetic anti-vibration, 125 mph speedometer with trip recorder and matching 10,000 rpm tachometer were fitted as standard onto a Metalastic bush mounted combined instrument bracket. Tachometer driven directly from the left end of the exhaust camshaft via a crankcase adaptor union, spade drive and drive cable.

Handlebars
⅞ in diameter chrome-plated Home and Overseas specification anti-vibration rubber Metalastic bush mounted in handlebar clamp bolts. Quick action twist-grip incorporating friction control fitted, and integral dipswitch and horn push. Ball-ended clutch and brake levers with built-in cable adjusters were specified as standard (no cut-out button fitted on this model).

Twinseat
Triumph design, two-level cushion seat covered in waterproof vynide, grey top, with white piping, black sides and grey lower rim band.

Finish
Frame:	Black
Forks:	Black
Mudguards:	Front – Alaskan white, gold stripe, black lined
	Rear – Alaskan white, gold stripe, black lined
Petrol tank:	Two-tone, gold top/Alaskan white lower half, black separating line
Oil tank:	Black
Switch panel:	Black

Extras
Quickly detachable rear wheel (46 teeth) pillion footrests, prop stand and steering lock were available as extra equipment.

U.S. Alternatives
All Models:	
Handlebars:	Overseas pattern including the necessary additional rubber and cap mounting washers and longer control cables.
	Twin rotor friction control twist-grip, ball-ended clutch and front brake control levers.
Clutch:	Armstrong cork clutch linings.
Front mudguard:	Less front number plate mounting hole piercings.
Air filter:	New combined single unit air filter feeding both carburetters on all models.

The USA east coast "R" version of the 1964 T120 road model

USA west coast version of the road model T120R

Colour:	As U.K. models.
T120R (Road Sports) – East Coast	
Speedmaster – West Coast:	
Fuel tank:	3½ (U.S.) gallons
Gearbox:	Standard ratio
	– 19T G/box drive sprocket
Wheels:	3.25 x 19 in Dunlop ribbed front
	4.00 x 18 in Dunlop K70 Gold Seal rear

Seat safety strap on West Coast models only.

USA east coast Bonneville model (T120C) for 1964, called the "Competition Sports"

T120C (Competition Sports – known as 'TT Special' on East Coast)

Fuel tank:	3½ (U.S.) gallons
Gearbox:	Standard ratio
	– 18 T G/box drive sprocket
Wheels:	3.25 x 19 in Dunlop Trials Universal front
	4.00 x 18 in Dunlop Trials Universal rear
Exhaust:	Upswept with two nonresonator silencers and leg guards.

Crankcase undershield as standard equipment and shorter stroke (2.2 in) suspension units.

T120C (TT Special – East and West Coast)

Engine unit:	11.2 : 1 compression ratio. 1³⁄₁₆ in diameter tapering to 1⅛ in diameter carburetter adaptors in the cylinder head. 1³⁄₁₆ in diameter choke Amal Monobloc carburetters.
Gearbox:	Standard ratio
	– 18 T Sprocket (East Coast)
	– 17 T Sprocket (West Coast)
Ignition:	Fitting the new Lucas 3ET (Energy Transfer) ignition coils under the fuel tank, in conjunction with the associated ET alternator stator, reduced range extended dwell auto advance twin contact breaker unit. The adjustable rotor having three pegged drive holes in the rear face suiting various conditions of competition usage (S – standard, M – mid and R – racing) required a peg-drive engine sprocket to match.
Spark plug:	Champion N58R standard equipment.
Cut-out:	New Lucas S55 cut-out switch fitted on handlebars.

The USA east coast version of the 1964 T120C 'TT' model

The USA west coast version differed only in the gearbox drive sprocket (17T) and in its black vinyl seat, top and sides with white piping and black lower rim trim band

Front forks:	Internal competition front fork damper units.
Rear Suspension:	Shorter stroke (2.2 in) suspension units.
Wheels:	3.50 x 19in Dunlop Universal K70 Gold Seal front
	4.00 x 18 in Dunlop Universal K70 Gold Seal rear
Mudguards:	Polished alloy front and rear.
Exhaust system:	Upswept system with straight-through extensions
	and mudguards.
Twinseat:	— Black top (West Coast only)

Crankcase undershield, tachometer only and less lighting were standard equipment on this model, whose power output was claimed to be 54 bhp at 6,500 rpm.

High Performance Components Listing
– As 1963.

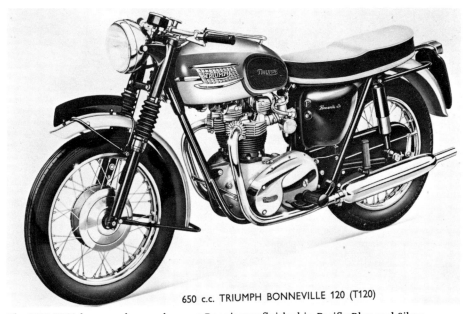

650 c.c. TRIUMPH BONNEVILLE 120 (T120)

The 1965 T120 home and general export Bonnie was finished in Pacific Blue and Silver

1965 model: Unit construction T120 model Bonneville 120
Commencing engine No. DU.13375

Models: T120 Bonneville 120 T120C Competition Sports
T120R Speedmaster T120C TT Special

Engine Unit
650cc unit construction vertical twin cylinder with two camshafts, cast iron cylinder block and 1⅛ in diameter splayed inlet port alloy cylinder head, 8.5 : 1 compression ratio pistons, and two Amal 1⅛ in diameter choke Monobloc carburetters. Carburetter inlet port adaptors were fitted with an induction balance pipe, and the cylinder head fitted with alloy exhaust pipe adaptors from engine No. DU.22682. **99**

Finned rocker boxes with locking rocker box caps were specified. The previous crankshaft with bolt-on central flywheel now incorporated the new TDC location slot facility, the crankshaft assembly being located to the drive (left) side, achieved by fitment of a new engine sprocket located against the drive side ball race, the new timing pinion providing the necessary clearance on the opposite bearing side. A timing plug in the timing side (right) crankcase provided access for the use of the TDC location tool, which locked the engine at TDC for initial ignition timing procedures. Dry sump lubrication with the plunger type pump continued, in association with a new oil pressure relief valve, deleting the tell-tale indicator button, one other previous source of oil leakage. A crankshaft mounted a.c. alternator rotor was fitted, and the exhaust camshaft driven Lucas 4CA twin contact breaker assembly was mounted in the timing cover.

Gearbox

Integral with the engine unit, the standard ratio shafts and gears were of hardened nickel and nickel chrome steel. Needle roller bearings supported the layshaft. A permanent welch washer replaced the bolt previously used to seal the drilling and boring access hole in the rear of the gearbox, giving access during manufacture to bore the gearbox camplate spindle bore. Thrust washer introduced together with a shorter kickstart ratchet pinion sleeve on the mainshaft, to obviate burring-up and consequent hang-up of the returning kickstart pedal. The positive stop, four-speed foot change continued.

Primary Transmission

Multi-plate clutch with Armstrong cork friction linings (under the original T1362 part number), with three vane clutch shock absorber. Renold ⅜ in pitch duplex primary chain lubricated by internal circulatory oil feed, the rear chain being lubricated by means of a metering jet in the primary chaincase. Longer alternator cable nut to prevent the alternator cable fouling the primary chain. Accessible filler and level plugs in the polished alloy cover.

Frame

Brazed single large diameter front downtube cradle type front frame with modified prop stand lug angle to prevent machine falling over on a rising road camber. The rear frame was modified to incorporate the fitting of a swinging arm bolt from the right side of the machine in lieu of the previous left side, to improve accessibility. Also a new bracket was fitted beneath the tank rail for horn mounting. The rear brake pedal operated from the inside of the new engine plate, giving a straight pull rear brake rod. Easy-lift centre stand with new pivot bolts and tab washers to prevent loosening off in continued use. Spacers were inserted into the battery box cross strap mounting rubbers to obviate over-tightening of the resilient mountings. Provision was made in the frame head lug for the insertion of a Nieman anti-theft lock, engaging in the slotted front fork stem.

Forks

Increased travel (1 inch) telescopic forks with longer stanchions, bottom outer members, and inner damping sleeves. Longer, softer external fork springs were also fitted, together with much neater rubber gaiters. Fitted with manual steering damper.

Fuel Tank

3 or 4 (Imp) gallon, all-steel, welded tank, rubber mounted and bolted front (x 2) and rear (x 1) were fitted, with quick release filler cap, chrome-plated parcel grid, chromed centre strip, and increased thickness stick-on knee grips on road models.

Oil Tank

Bolted at the top to two rubber mounted frame cross straps, and with a rubber insulated lower spigot mounting. Engine breather pipe connected to the anti-froth tower via a connector 'T' piece.

Rear Suspension Units

Swinging arm rear suspension, with Girling hydraulically damped rear suspension unit, adjustable for varying loads.

Brakes

Front:	Full width 8 in diameter finned cast iron hub, with single leading shoe drum brake.
Rear:	7 in diameter cast iron drum integral with rear chain sprocket (46 teeth).

Fully floating shoes fitted on both front and rear brakes, with an adjustable front fulcrum pin, and front brake cable abutment, replacing the previous abutment incorporated in the front fork sliding member.

Wheels

Triumph designed 3.25 x 18 in ribbed front, and 3.50 x 18 in Dunlop K70 Gold Seal on the rear wheels. Spokes and rims were plated. In conjunction with the new 1965 front fork, the front wheel spindle was amended to suit the new front forks. Both the standard and Q.D. rear wheels incorporated new wheel bearing grease retainer discs and felt sealing washers, the rear brake cam levers and return springs being amended to suit the new rear brake straight pull rod. The Q.D. wheel itself deleted the taper roller bearings in favour of ball journal bearings.

Mudguards

Painted steel mudguards fitted front and rear.

Exhaust System

1½ in diameter downswept exhaust pipes incorporating additional tabs enabling them to be braced across the front of the engine. Resonator silencers similarly braced across the nose clips.

Air Filter

Single unit air filter box with replaceable element feeding both carburetter intakes, available when required.

Electrical Equipment

Lucas 6 volt a.c. generator system, rectified to d.c. feeding the MLZ9E 12 ampere/hour 6 volt battery via a silicone rectifier and 2AR ammeter in the chromed headlamp, incorporating a 30/24 watt pre-focus bulb. Ignition controlled by two Lucas MA6 ignition coils rubber mounted onto the frame beneath the fuel tank and operated by the exhaust driven camshaft. Lucas 4CA twin contact breaker and auto advance unit mounted in the timing cover housing. A 25 ampere fuse was incorporated in the charging circuit. Lucas 88 SA (multi-pin plug/socket) type lighting and ignition switches were installed (lighting uppermost) in the switch panel on the left side of the machine. EMG starting was available in the event of a discharged battery. A combined stop/tail rear light was fitted as standard. The Lucas 8H hooter was mounted (facing sideways) on the lower frame tank rail, under the fuel tank.

Speedometer and Tachometer

Smiths 125 mph anti-vibration magnetic type speedometer with trip recorder fitted in conjunction with a matching 10,000 rpm tachometer on a Metalastic mounted instrument bracket. Tachometer driven directly from the end of the exhaust camshaft via a crankcase adaptor union, spade drive and drive cable.

Handlebars

New shaped ⅞ in diameter chrome-plated Home and Overseas handlebars to provide a claimed 'more comfortable' ride, which were anti-vibration rubber Metalastic bush mounted in the handlebar clamp bolts. Quick-action twist-grip incorporating friction control fitted, and integral dipswitch and horn push. Clutch and brake levers with built-in cable adjusters were specified as standard (no cut-out button fitted as standard to this model).

Twinseat

Triumph design, two-level cushioned seat, covered in waterproof vynide, grey top, white piping, black sides and grey lower rim band fitted to all road machines.

Finish

Frame:	Black
Forks:	Black
Mudguards:	Front – Silver, Pacific blue stripe, gold lined
	Rear – Silver, Pacific blue stripe, gold lined
Petrol tank:	Two-tone Pacific blue top/silver lower half, gold separating line.
Oil tank:	Black
Switch panel:	Black

Extras

Quickly detachable rear wheel (46 teeth), pillion footrests, prop stand and steering lock were available as extra equipment.

U.S. Alternatives

All models:	
Handlebars:	New shaped Overseas pattern handlebars to provide a more comfortable ride. Ball-ended clutch and front brake control levers.
Stop/tail light:	New type Lucas 679
Colour:	As U.K. models

1965 USA east coast T120R model

T120R (Road Sports – East Coast, Speedmaster – West Coast)

Fuel tank:	3½ (U.S.) gallons
Gearbox:	Standard ratio
	– 19T G/box drive sprocket
Wheels:	3.25 x 19 in Dunlop ribbed front
	4.00 x 18 in Dunlop K70 Gold Seal rear
Silencers:	New smaller streamlined pattern
(mufflers)	
Air filter:	1 x combined unit feeding both carburetters
Mudguards:	Painted steel (front and rear) – East Coast
	Polished alloy (front and rear) – West Coast

Seat safety strap on West Coast models only.

T120C (Competition Sports – known as 'TT Special on East Coast)

Fuel tank:	3½ (U.S.) gallons
Gearbox:	Standard ratio
	– 18 T G/box drive sprocket
Wheels:	3.25 x 19 in Dunlop Trials Universal front
	4.00 x 18 in Dunlop Trials Universal rear
Front forks:	Heavy duty front fork springs
	Longer internal damper units
Exhaust:	Upswept with non-resonator mufflers
Air filter:	1 x combined unit feeding both carburetters
Footrests:	45° upward folding footrests (to comply with U.S. Competition Regulations)
Mudguards:	Painted steel (front and rear) – East Coast
	Heavy duty polished alloy with beaded edges for durability – West
Cut-out:	Lucas S55 on handlebars

Crankcase undershield as standard equipment.

USA west coast T120 R road model in 1965, fitted with the normal twinseat "safety strap", a legal requirement of the period

T120C (TT Special – East and West Coast)

Engine unit:	New 11 : 1 compression ratio pistons fitted for use with oversized inlet valves and Jomo (Johnson Motors) racing camshafts.
	1³⁄₁₆ in choke diameter Amal Monobloc carburetter adaptors, tapering to 1⅛ in diameter in the cylinder head.
Gearbox:	Standard ratio

103

1965 T120C 'TT' Special, supplied to both east and west coasts of USA, the west coast version was fitted with black vinyl twinseat, and both with 1¾ inch diameter low-level tucked-in, open, racing exhaust pipes

The USA east coast T120C competition sports model for 1965. The competition version followed the normal practice of specifying a black seat

	– 17 T G/box drive sprocket
Ignition:	E.T. (Energy Transfer)
Spark plug:	Champion N58R
Cut-out:	Lucas S55 on handlebars
Front forks:	Heavy duty fork springs
	Longer internal damper units
Wheels:	3.50 x 19 in Dunlop Universal K70 Gold Seal – front

	4.00 x 18 in Dunlop Universal K70 Gold Seal – rear
Mudguards:	Heavy duty polished alloy with beaded edges
Exhaust system:	New low-level tucked-in open racing pipes, 1.75 in diameter.
Air filter:	1 x combined unit feeding both carburetters
Twinseat:	Black top (West Coast only)
Footrests:	45° upward folding footpeg (to comply with U.S. Competition Regulations)

Crankcase undershield tachometer only and 'less lighting' were standard equipment on this model.

High Performance Components Listing
– As 1963.

The 1966 home and general export model T120 in Grenadier Red and Alaskan White finish. The immediate identifying features for this model were the flanged full width hub and white handlebar grips

1966 model: Unit construction T120 model Bonneville 120
Commencing engine No. DU.24875

Models: T120 Bonneville 120
*   T120R Bonneville Road Sports T120TT Bonneville TT Special*

Engine Unit:
The 650cc unit construction vertical twin cylinder power unit continued with the previous specification twin camshafts, cast iron cylinder block and 1⅛ in diameter splayed inlet port cylinder head although new Red Spot inner and outer valve springs and associated bottom valve spring cup were fitted. These 105

springs had previously been designed to mate with the Dowson ramp camshaft to provide 'quiet performance' on the 6T model Thunderbird, but they also provided a most satisfactory surge/bounce free characteristic on the latest Bonnie.

Problems were experienced towards the end of the previous season with subsequent loosening of the aluminium exhaust pipe adaptors in the cylinder head which led to reintroduction of the previous steel adaptors from DU.39464. 9.1 compression ratio pistons were now fitted in conjunction with the previously specified twin Amal 1⅛ in diameter choke Monobloc carburetters, with inlet port adaptors fitted with an induction balance pipe. Finned rocker boxes with locking caps continued. A new flywheel of reduced weight (2½ lb), but maintaining 85% balance factor by amending the periphery to a stepped cross section was fitted to the crankcase using longer flywheel bolts. The crankshaft location reverted to timing (right) side, retaining the primary chain drive sprocket introduced last year, together with the associated timing pinion. This was achieved by inserting the previous clamping washer (E3300) between the new pinion and timing side bearing inner spool to clamp the crankshaft over to that side, and by fitting a heavier duty single lipped roller bearing on the drive side. The TDC location facility continued in the timing (right) side crankcase, which now incorporated additional drillways to feed an oil supply (at engine pressure) for the timing cover metering dowel to the crankcase/cylinder base flange joint from where the supply was taken to drillways in the exhaust cam follower tappet guide block. A dowel was later introduced (at engine No. DU.42399) into the crankcase/cylinder base flange joint, to obviate any possible oil pressure loss in the event of a cylinder base oil leak. Simultaneously, 1⅛ in radius (High Performance) 'R' type sports cam followers (tappets) were introduced onto the inlet camshaft location and 1⅛ in radius oil fed tappets into the exhaust.

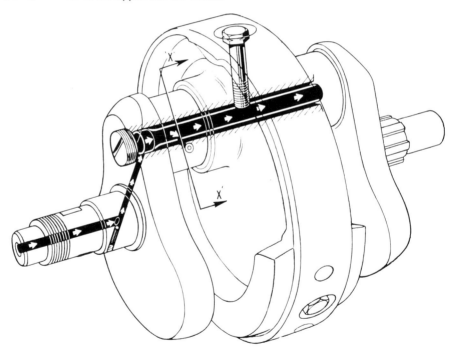

1966/8 narrow flywheel assembly. Fully interchangeable and with the indentical 85% balance factor. The overall flywheel effect was reduced to provide a more immediate engine response characteristic

The new oil fed exhaust and inlet tappet guide blocks were designed to be used in conjunction with the new straight walled and flanged pushrod cover tubes, which fitted into the cylinder head at the top, and seated in the silicone rubber washer, retained in a cup washer, itself located over the tappet guide block at the base flange. A new induction heat treated intermediate wheel complete with bronze bush from which the pinion teeth had been cut and subsequently heat treated was specified.

The crankshaft mounted a.c. generator continued to be fitted for 1966, and no changes were made to the Lucas 4CA contact breaker and auto advance mechanism fitted in the timing cover even though the elctrical system itself was converted to 12 volts d.c.

Gearbox
Integral with the engine unit, the standard ratio shafts and gears were of hardened nickel and nickel chrome steel, needle rollers supporting the layshaft. Internal changes were the deletion of the layshaft speedometer drive pinion, and cable take-off point in the gearbox inner cover. A new, longer, kick-start pedal was specified to assist in starting with the high compression ratio pistons. The positive stop, four-speed foot change continued unchanged.

Primary Transmission
A new large diameter adjusting screw was incorporated in the clutch outer pressure plate after DU.31168 in the multi-plate clutch, which incorporated the engine drive shock absorber. Although a CEI threaded self locknut was specified for the 1966 clutch assembly deleting the tab washer, this was not to be implemented on production until 1967 when UNF threads were introduced. The rear chain oiler facility from the rear of the primary inner chaincase was discontinued by substitution of the metering jet by a screw plug. The Renold ⅜ in pitch duplex primary chain lubricated by internal circulatory oil feed, continued to be fitted. The polished alloy cover specified accessible filler and level plugs.

Frame
The brazed cradle type single large diameter front downtube front frame now incorporated an entirely new head lug casting, with a revised steering head angle (65° to 62°) to improve the high speed steering characteristic. Also incorporated, in response to both public and police utilisation demands, were fairing attachment lugs. At the same time the rear swinging arm fork had the timing side fork moved out by ¼ in (i.e. from 3½ in to 3¾ in centres). The rear frame itself was modified by the incorporation of two round pegs on the right side, to accept the new 12 volt battery carrier mounted on a new type of frame cross strap incorporating tubular end and frame peg spigot rubber mountings. The new switch panel accommodating the new Yale type barrel ignition switch was attached at the top to the threaded studs welded to the rubber mounted battery carrier cross straps. Easy-lift centre stand continued to be fitted.

Front Forks
A new bottom fork lug allowing a tighter turning circle (after engine No. DU.27672) and with the new plastic damping sleeves (introduced after DU.31119) the Triumph embossed manual steering damper continued as standard equipment.

Fuel Tank
New, slimmer 3 or 4 (Imp) or 2½ (U.S.) gallon all-steel welded fuel tank, rubber mounted and bolted (x 2) front and (x 1) rear wcre fitted, with quick release filler cap, chromed centre strip parcel grid and a new design of tank badges.

Oil Tank
Suspended at the top from two spigot rubber mounts, (onto which the battery case cross themselves were bolted) and restrained by a lower rubber spigot mounting, the new 6 pint oil tank featured an adjustable rear chain oiler metering screw and feed in the filler cap necks.

Rear Suspension
The rear swinging arm suspension was controlled by Girling rear suspension units, adjustable for varying loads.

Brakes
A new full width hub drum brake was fitted at the front incorporating 8 in diameter single leading shoes which provided over 40% increase in braking area. The new 7 in diameter cast iron brake drum on the standard rear wheel incorporated a new bolt-on (46 teeth) rear sprocket, whilst on the Q.D. wheel sprocket remained integral with the drum.

Wheels

Triumph designed 3.25 x 18 in ribbed front, and 3.50 x 18 in Dunlop K7 Gold Seal tyres were fitted to the rear wheels. The spokes and rims were painted. Both the standard and the Q.D. rear wheels were modified on the right side hub spoke flange to accept the slotted drive sleeve to accommodate the speedometer drive gearbox.

Mudguards

Both front and rear mudguards were of painted steel.

Exhaust System

Continuing with the basic 1½ in diameter downswept exhaust system, the pipes and silencers were both braced across the front and between the silencer nose clips.

Air Filter

The single air filter element feeding both carburetters remained standard equipment on home and general export models.

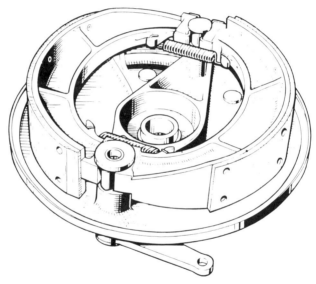

The 1966 single leading shoe front brake assembly, illustrating the wider shoes providing 44% greater brake lining area and increased stopping power

Electrical Equipment

12 volt Zener diode voltage controlled electrical equipment was fitted for the first time, feeding two Lucas MKZ9E batteries (a single Lucas PUZ5A after engine No. DU.32994 – requiring a further amendment to the battery carrier, carrier lining and cross straps). The previous silicone rectifier was fitted (but mounted on an improved bracket after engine No. DU.27007), and the 2AR ammeter continued in the chromed headlamp, which now incorporated both ignition warning (green) and headlamp main beam warning light (red) after engine No. DU.31565. The ignition coils introduced were Lucas MA12 rubber mounted as before on the frame underneath the fuel tank and operated by the Lucas 4CA twin contact breaker and auto advance unit driven by the exhaust camshaft, and housed in the timing cover. Lucas 88SA (multi-pin and socket) type lighting switch was fitted, but a new ignition switch incorporating a Yale type key and barrel lock was fitted in the new left side switch panel. A combined stop/tail rear light was fitted as standard equipment. The earthing tag was removed from

under the contact face of the Zener diode to the rear of the heat sink after DU.30800, and the new right angle heat sink plate fitted after engine No. DU.32898 due to early problems of 'heat-soak' experienced on the West Coast of the U.S.A., causing premature failure.

Speedometer and Tachometer
The previous 1600 cable rpm speedometer continued, but was now driven from the rear wheel speedometer drive gearbox. The new tachometer was driven from a 2 : 1 right angle drive gearbox, with a right-hand adaptor thread installation into the left side crankcase, driven by the exhaust camshaft.

Handlebars
Metalastic bush mounted, Home and Overseas handlebars were mounted in clamp bolts, and now incorporated as standard the Lucas S55 cut-out button. (Lucas 35601, not to be confused with the S55 cut-out button Lucas 31071 fitted to a.c. magneto machines, which connected both the ignition coil primaries together, whereas the coil ignition cut-out button simultaneously earthed both ignition coil primaries). New white rubber handlebar grips were fitted.

Twinseat
Of Triumph design, the two-level cushion seat was covered in waterproof vynide. It had a grey top, with white piping, black sides and grey lower rim band fitted to all road machines.

Finish
Frame:	Black
Forks:	Black
Mudguards:	Front: Alaskan white, Grenadier red stripe, gold lined
	Rear: Alaskan white, Grenadier red stripe, gold lined
Petrol tank:	Two-tone, Grenadier red top/Alaskan white lower half, gold separating line
Oil tank:	Black
Switch panel:	Black

Extras
Quickly detachable rear wheel (46 teeth), pillion footrests, prop stand and steering lock were available as extra equipment.

U.S. Alternatives
Both models were now fitted with the new sporty look slim fuel tank and no longer specified a fuel tank parcel grid as standard equipment.

Models: T120R Road Sports – East Coast; Speedmaster – West Coast

Fuel tank:	2½ (U.S.) gallons, finish as U.K. models.
Engine unit:	Exhaust camshaft E.5047 (E3134 form) after DU.31119.
	'R' specification inlet and exhaust cam followers (tappets).
	Cylinder head – 1³⁄₁₆ in diameter inlet adaptors tapering to 1⅛ in diameter after engine No. DU.29738.
Gearbox:	Standard ratio
	– 19 T G/box sprocket
Carburetter:	1³⁄₁₆ in diameter choke Amal Monobloc 389/95 (No. 2 needle position and No. 4 slide after engine No. DU.34086).
Front forks:	Alternative fork crown and stem lug to allow fork turning circle to suit 2½ gallon fuel tank.

The T120/R Bonneville Road Sports

Both east and west coast versions of the 1966 T120 R model were identical except the west coast model additionally specified the statutory seat safety strap. The tank and guards were Alaskan White with central Grenadier Red stripes, lined Gold

	Chromed top nut fitted in place of steering damper unit.
Wheels:	3.25 x 19 in Dunlop ribbed front
	4.00 x 18 in Dunlop K70 Gold Seal rear
Air filters:	(East) – 2 x 1³⁄₁₆ in diameter inlet pancake air filters.
	(West) – 1 x combined single unit feeding both carburetters.
Mudguards:	Stainless steel, front and rear.
Mufflers:	Straight-through sports muffler.
Stop/tail light:	New alloy tail lamp casting for Lucas 679 tail light.
Ignition coils:	Siba 32,000/1

Seat Safety strap specified for West Coast models only.

T120C (TT Special) – East and West Coast

Fuel tank:	2½ (U.S.) gallons, finish as U.K. models
Engine unit:	11 : 1 compression ratio
Gearbox:	Standard ratio
	19 T drive sprocket
Carburetters:	1³⁄₁₆ in diameter choke Amal Monobloc 389/95
Ignition:	E.T. (Energy Transfer)
Spark plugs:	Champion N58R
Handlebars:	Early type bar (H1511) fitted Lucas S55 cut-out (31071) button.
Wheels:	3.50 x 19 in Dunlop Universal K70 Gold Seal front
	4.00 x 18 in Dunlop Universal K70 Gold Seal rear

The illustration depicts the 1966 T120C 'TT' models supplied to both east and west coasts, USA distribution networks. The east coast version had Alaskan White fenders, lined Grenadier Red with Gold separating line; the west coast version had polished alloy fenders. Both had 2½ US gallon gasoline tanks in Alaskan White with central Grenadier Red 'racing' stripes. This particular photograph appears to depict an alternative twinseat with grey top for the west coast, normally specified "all black" for competition use

Mudguards:	Painted steel (East Coast)
	Polished alloy (West Coast)
Exhaust system:	1.75 in diameter low level tucked-in, open racing pipes.
Air filter:	1 x combined single unit feeding both carburetters.
Twinseat:	All black cover and top (West Coast).

Crankcase undershield, tachometer only and 'less lighting' were standard equipment on this model.

1967 model: Unit construction T120 model Bonneville 120
Commencing engine No. DU.44394

Models: T120 Bonneville T120
    T120R Bonneville   T120TT Bonneville TT Special

Engine
The engine unit remained unchanged as a 650cc unit construction vertical twin cylinder, maintaining the previous specification high performance inlet camshaft and 'R' type cam followers (tappets). but for

1967 home model Bonneville with the quilted seat top and in Aubergine and Alaskan White paint finish

1967 a copper plated (E3134 form) high performance camshaft was additionally specified for the exhaust but continuing with the previously specified (oil fed) ¾ in radius cam follower. The standard home and general export 1⅛ in diameter splayed inlet port alloy cylinder head was fitted in conjunction with Amal Monobloc type 389/95 1⅛ in diameter choke carburetters (240 main jets were incorporated after engine No. DU.52578). However, the new 30 mm choke diameter Amal Concentric carburetter type 930 were fitted (and located by H.T. bolts and self lock nuts) after engine No. DU.59320. The parallel 1⅛ in diameter inlet port adaptors were connected by a rubber balance pipe to aid carburation and idling characteristics. New 9 : 1 compression ratio Hepolite pistons were fitted together with new, heavy duty increased cross section RR56 polished alloy connecting rods, with plain big-end shell bearing inserts.

In the continuing search to eliminate exhaust camshaft wear, the oil pressure fed exhaust cam followers (tappets) were now fed via a new metering feed dowel, which introduced a filter gauze at the timing cover bolt, and a 'jiggle pin' in the metering jet, to obviate any possibility of blockage due to obstruction. This feature was deleted in favour of timed tappets after engine No. DU.63043. Rubber 'O' rings were also introduced at the base of the tappet guide blocks from DU.63241 onwards.

A new oil pump with increased scavenge plunger capacity was introduced to maintain a lower general level of residual crankcase oil. The crankshaft mounted a.c. generator rotor continued, but a new 160° dwell auto advance unit cam was incorporated (to overcome a random spark phenomenon on 12 volt machines) in the Lucas 4CA contact breaker unit from engine No. DU.51771.

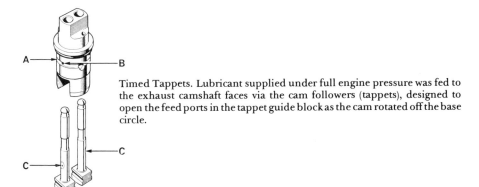

Timed Tappets. Lubricant supplied under full engine pressure was fed to the exhaust camshaft faces via the cam followers (tappets), designed to open the feed ports in the tappet guide block as the cam rotated off the base circle.

Gearbox

The only change in the integral gearbox unit and components for 1967 models was the elimination of sharp corners on the layshaft splines to eliminate the occasional competition activity fractures, and the deletion of alternate engagement dogs on the mainshaft second gear from engine No. DU.64758 to DU.64858. Plastic gasket was applied to seal the high gear splines against oil seepage past the gearbox sprocket.

Primary Transmission

The old clutch nut tab washer was replaced by a new CEI threaded lock nut after DU.48114. By far the most important change however was the fitment of the entirely new Lucas encapsulated stator, ensuring a complete and final end to all the previously experienced stator problems, from engine No. DU.58565 onwards.

Frame

Threaded steering stops, to allow variation in the fork lock angle to suit the new range of slimmer fuel tanks was introduced onto the existing brazed type single large diameter front downtube front frame. An extension on the left side of the top of the headlug accommodated the location peg of the new fork steering lock now fitted to the front fork top crown lug. The tank mounting lug and bottom lug were tapped UNF threads. The Easy-lift centre stand continued as an essential feature.

Forks

A new fork top lug was introduced to carry the new Yale type barrel lock, which in use engaged a peg into a mating hole in the frame headlug top flange. An oil sealing 'O' ring was fitted into an additional groove machined into the top of the threads in the dust excluder sleeve nuts to prevent oil seepage down the threads. Gaiter spring clips replaced the previous worm drive clips. The manual steering damper remained standard equipment.

Fuel Tank

2½ (U.S.), 3 and 4 (Imp) gallon all-steel welded fuel tanks, rubber mounted (x 2) front and (x 1) rear were fitted with the previous quick release filler cap, chromed centre strip, chromed parcel grid and tank badges.

Oil Tank

The rocker spindle oil-feed pipe reverted to a 'take-off' pipe below the 6 pint oil tank return line from DU.55772.

Brakes

Front:	Full width 8 in diameter finned cast iron hub, with single leading shoe front brake.
Rear:	7 in diameter cast iron drum integral with the rear chain sprocket.

Fully floating shoes were fitted to both front and rear brakes.

Wheels

A 19 in diameter (Triumph design) front wheel (3.0 x 19 in Dunlop ribbed front tyre) was fitted to home and general export machines for the first time since 1962. 3.50 x 18 in Dunlop Universal K70 Gold Seal were fitted to the rear.

Mudguards

Painted steel front and rear mudguards were fitted.

Exhaust System

Two short exhaust pipe braces were fitted to the pipe front mounting brackets bolted to the front crankcase mounting bolts.

Air Filter

The 'big-box' single air filter was dropped in favour of two single pancake air filters on general export machines when required. Air filters were not specified for U.K. models.

Electrical Equipment

Lucas a.c. generator equipment continued to be specified, rectified and Zener diode controlled to the 12 volt Lucas PUZ5A battery, via the 2AR ammeter in the chromed headlamp, which now carried the lighting switch, the ignition warning (green) light, and the headlamp main beam warning light (red). The ignition switch remained in the left side switch panel. A louder hooter (Lucas 6H) was fitted.

Instruments

The new Smiths 150 mph speedometer (1600 cable rpm) was fitted for 1967. A Stat-O-Seal washer was interposed between the tachometer drive gearbox and the crankcase, to obviate oil seepage and any tendency for the drive box to loosen off in service.

Handlebars

The Metalastic bush mounted handlebar clamp arrangement continued for the new season for both Home and overseas bars. The U.S. handlebars required additional stiffening washers to control the overall flexibility of the system.

Twinseat

A new Triumph design grey quilted top was introduced, with white piping, black sidewalls, and grey lower rim trim band. The rear of the seat now had a tip-up effect to assist in preventing the passenger from sliding rearwards.

Finish

Frame:	Black
Forks:	Black
Mudguards:	Front – Aubergine with Alaskan White stripe, lined Gold
	Rear – Aubergine with Alaskan White stripe, lined Gold
Petrol tank:	Two-tone, Aubergine top/Alaskan White lower half, Gold separating line
Oil tank:	Black
Switch panel:	Black

Extras

The quickly detachable rear wheel, pillion footrests, prop stand and fork steering lock remained available as extra equipment.

U.S. Alternatives

Fuel tank top parcel grids were no longer fitted to U.S. T120 models.
T120R Bonneville (52 claimed bhp at 6,500 rpm – straight-through exhaust system).

Fuel tank:	2¹/2 (U.S.) gallons – Two-tone Aubergine top. Gold lower half, White separating line.
Engine unit:	Hepolite 9 : 1 pistons. Cylinder head 1³⁄₁₆ in diameter inlet adaptors tapering to 1⅛ in diameter inlet ports.
Gearbox:	Standard ratio. 19 T G/box drive sprocket.
Carburetters:	1³⁄₁₆ in diameter choke Amal Monobloc 389/90 replaced by Amal Concentric type 930 after DU.59320.
Air filters:	2 x separate pancake air filters (coarse felt element)

The USA T120R model as supplied to both east and west coasts, with stainless steel fenders. Tank top parcel grids were no longer fitted to US T120 models

Front forks:	Alternative fork crown and stem lug to allow fork turning circle to suit 2½ gallon fuel tank. Chromed domed nut in place of steering damper.
Wheels:	3.25 x 19 in Dunlop ribbed front. 4.00 x 18 in Dunlop Universal K70 Gold Seal rear.
Mudguards:	New stainless steel, front and rear.
Mufflers:	Straight-through sports mufflers.
Ignition coils:	Siba 32000/1
Stop/tail light:	Lucas type 679 with alloy casting.

Seat safety strap specified for West Coast models only.

T120TT Bonneville TT Special (54 claimed bhp at 6,500 rpm, straight-through exhaust system.

Fuel tank:	2½ (U.S.) gallons – Two-tone Aubergine top. Gold lower half, White separating line.
Engine unit:	Hepolite 11.2 : 1 pistons. 1³⁄₁₆ in diameter inlet port adaptors tapering to 1⅛ in diameter in cylinder head.
Gearbox:	Standard gear ratio. 17 T G/box sprocket.
Carburetters:	1³⁄₁₆ in diameter Amal Monobloc 389/90 replaced by Amal Concentric type 930 after DU.59320.
Ignition:	Energy Transfer
Spark plug:	Champion N58R
Wheels:	3.50 x 19 in Dunlop Universal K70 Gold Seal front 4.00 x 18 in Dunlop Universal K70 Gold Seal rear.
Mudguards:	New stainless steel front and rear.
Exhaust system:	1¾ in diameter low level tucked-in, open racing pipes.
Air filters:	2 x separate pancake type air filters (coarse felt elements).
Twinseat:	Quilted vinyl, with all black top and cover.

Crankcase undershield, tachometer only and 'less lighting' were standard equipment on this model.

This was the last year of the T120C TT model for the U.S.A.

Two views of the 1967 T120C 'TT' model, in Aubergine and Gold with Black quilted top twinseat and stainless steel fenders. This was the last year of the manufacture of the Triumph 'TT' model

Left-hand view of the 1968 T120 Bonneville model for the home and general export market, illustrating the twin leading shoe front brake and associated fluted full width hub drum cover. The colour scheme was Hi-Fi Scarlet tank top with Silver lower half and Gold separating lines

1968 model: Unit construction T120 model Bonneville 120
Commencing engine No. DU.66246

Models: T120 Bonneville 120
T120R Bonneville Road Sports

Engine

A number of small but important detail changes took place for 1968 on the otherwise unaltered basic specification of the 650cc Bonneville unit construction vertical twin cylinder power unit. High performance camshafts continued to be fitted, the exhaust camshaft now being oil fed by means of a regulated high pressure oil flow, controlled by timed tappets (i.e. cam followers incorporating machined flats allowing oil under pressure to be fed to the camshaft face at a pre-determined location immediately prior to initial cam lift). The 1⅛ in diameter splayed inlet port alloy cylinder head as fitted for the previous four years continued to be fitted, but now specified Green Spot outer valve springs (providing a 10% increase in fitted load at valve fully open, but maintaining the original loading when closed.) Previously, oil supplied to the rocker spindles was also fed down the rocker arm drillways to the rocker arm ball pins, locating in the pushrod top cups. From engine No. DU.78400 the assembly of the ball pins was reversed (rotated 180°) to cut off this feed, in order to maintain maximum supply to the exhaust camshaft. At DU.79965 the rocker arms were left undrilled, which has the additional advantage of strengthening the rocker arms themselves.

30 mm diameter choke Amal Concentric type 930 carburetters were fitted, the 1⅛ in diameter adaptors being interconnected by a rubber balance pipe. 9 : 1 Hepolite pistons incorporated a reinforced crown for 1968, no change being introduced to the RR56 polished alloy connecting rods, or the plain big-end shell bearing inserts. The crankshaft was modified to incorporate three different sequential conditions of TDC/38° BTC notches in the first 1800 machines, culminating in reinstatement to the rear of the cylinder barrel at DU.74052.

117

The cast iron cylinder barrel was retained using 12 point cylinder base nuts, providing for the first time adequate spanner clearance and accessibility, hence accurate cylinder barrel tightening down torque.

No change was made for 1968 to the crankshaft mounted alternator rotor assembly, but the new Lucas 6CA contact breaker assembly with independently positioned and adjustable twin contact breaker sets was introduced (now also requiring a UNF threaded extractor bolt) to which was subsequently added felt lubricating wicks after DU.82146. A new deeper timing cover was fitted to accommodate the new C.B. assembly.

1. Black/yellow
2. Pillar bolt
3. Black/white
4. Secondary bracket screw
5. Eccentric screw
6. Contact locking screw
7. Contact eccentric adjusting screw
8. Lubricating pad

Lucas 6CA Contact Breaker assembly. Each pair of contact breaker points were capable of being set individually, each point's baseplate adjustable on the main baseplate, and the main baseplate adjustable within the contact breaker housing

Gearbox

Changes to the gearbox included an extended length gearbox mainshaft (10 63/64 in to 11 19/64 in) to allow the incorporation of UNF threads at both ends. The associated layshaft deleted the earlier speedometer drive gear shaft bore and locating peg cross drillway. A new mainshaft high gear with 'extended nose' enveloped the previous longer bronze bush, requiring a new primary inner cover plate and associated oil seal.

Primary Transmission

In addition to a new clutch lock absorber spider (requiring the new UNF self lock nut and use of a UNF threaded extractor D652/3), and the addition of the new rear cover plate and oil seal, the most important development was the incorporation of an inspection cover in the primary chaincase outer cover. This feature, used in conjunction with the service tool D2014 (stroboscope timing plate) and with the introduction of two scribed lines on the rotor, allowed stroboscopic timing to be achieved without recourse to fitting an external timing disc by the owner or fitter. A permanent fixed pointer indicating 38° BTC (ignition fully advanced) was incorporated after engine No. DU.83021.

Frame

A new front frame incorporating a new headlug with extended steering lock shelf (to prevent the possibility of riding off with the lock peg still engaged) and a new swinging arm lug was introduced. The rear frame was modified to include spigot pegs. These were to mount the new left side panel, now doubling up as the toolbox, located and held at the forward top flange by a threaded plastic knob. (Later to require a 'click spring' retainer to prevent loosening off, with resultant loss of the panel complete with toolkit!) The new swinging arm had heavier corner fillets, and thicker section tube (14 SWG to 12 SWG) was used from DU.81196, providing a considerable increase in rigidity. To aid greasing of the spindle a 1 $\frac{1}{16}$ in diameter breather hole was introduced into the cover plate, allowing the air to escape. The Easy-lift centre stand continued as previously, but the prop stand lost its foot pressing in favour of a curved extension added to the stamping itself.

Forks

The new fork assembly for 1968 was almost externally indentical with the previous year's model, apart from the left hand top headlamp mounting cover, now incorporating the ignition switch housing. The most important internal change however was the introduction of the 'shuttle valve' controlled oil damping system. (N.B. The first series DU.68636 had CEI threaded components, whereas the subsequent models had UNF threaded stanchions, bearing and cap nuts.) An interim condition of sintered iron stanchion bushes was discontinued in favour of the original sintered bronze bushes.

Fuel Tank

2½ (U.S.) and 4 (Imp) gallon all-steel welded fuel tanks were fitted, 3-point rubber mounted with studs and nuts replacing the previous (x2) front bolts after DU.77670. Thicker stick-on knee grips were introduced, Stat-O-Seal washers were fitted between the fuel taps and the petrol tank boss, to allow a petrol-tight seal whilst aligning the tap levers. The chrome parcel grid continued to be fitted as standard equipment.

Oil Tank

The rubber mounted oil tank incorporated a rocker spindle feed pipe branch in the return oil supply, continuing up to a metered supply to the rear chain, controlled by a metering screw in the filler cap neck.

Rear Suspension

The rear suspension swinging arm was controlled by Girling hydraulically damped suspension units.

Brakes

Front: Full width 8 in diameter finned cast iron hub, with the new twin leading shoe front brake and with an air scoop incorporated in the front brake anchor plate.

Right side view of the 1968 Home T120 model illustrating the twin leading shoe, full width hub front brake, new knee grips, pancake air filters and 'finned egg' Zener diode heat sink on the front forks

Rear: 7 in diameter cast iron drum on the standard rear wheel incorporated a bolt-on (46T) steel rear sprocket whilst the Q.D. wheel sprocket remained integral with the drum.

New fully floating shoes were fitted to both front and rear wheels. A split pin was added to the front brake cable abutment at DU.70083 to prevent the cable jumping out, if badly adjusted. The cover plate fitted to the 1968 front wheel drum was fluted.

Wheels
3.00 x 19 in diameter ribbed front wheel and tyre were fitted, with 3.50 x 18 in diameter Dunlop K70 Gold Seal Universal rear.

Mudguards
Painted steel front and rear mudguards were fitted with a longer front mudguard from DU.81709 onwards.

Exhaust System
Externally similar to the previous year, the 1968 silencers had redesigned internal baffles to prevent loosening off and eliminate internal rattling.

Air Filters
Two separate pancake air filters with paper elements were introduced as standard equipment.

Electrical Equipment
Major changes took place in the electrical equipment. The Lucas RM19 alternator continuing, rectified to d.c. and 12 volt Zener diode controlled, the diode now being fitted to the 'finned egg' heat sink, mounted onto the front fork middle lug. A new headlamp unit with a three position toggle lever switch for lighting control was fitted in conjunction with the repositioned ignition switch, installed in a new housing in the left fork cover. A new silicone damped Lucas ammeter was fitted in the headlamp shell.

In conjunction with the new Lucas 6CA contact breaker assembly, now featuring independently positioned and adjustable contact breaker point sets (eliminating the accommodation of adjacent condensers), an external twin condenser was now located beneath the fuel tank forward mounting.

Instruments
The 150 mph (Smiths) speedometer and tachometer equipment continued as previously without change.

Handlebars
No change whatsoever was made in the handlebar and control equipment from the previous year's model.

Twinseat
A new twinseat with thicker cushion effect, and incorporating external hinges made from pressings superseded the previous seat (which utilised internal forged steel hinge brackets). The tip-up rear effect was retained, as was the internal fixing bracketry to enable fitment of the optional safety strap, as and when required. Grey quilted top, white piping, black sidewalls and chromed plastic beading lower rim trim was introduced for 1968.

Finish

Frame:	Black
Forks:	Black
Mudguards:	Front – silver with Hi-Fi scarlet stripe, lined gold
	Rear – silver with Hi-Fi scarlet stripe, lined gold
Petrol tank:	Two-tone, Hi-Fi scarlet top/silver lower half with gold separating line
Oil tank:	Black
Toolbox cover:	Black

Extras
The quickly detachable rear wheel, pillion footrests, prop stand and fork steering lock continued as optional extra equipment.

The 1968 American T120R model supplied to both coasts were fitted with fork gaiters as standard and chromed safety rail bolted to the underside of the rear of the twinseat

U.S. Alternatives
T120R Bonneville Model

Fuel tank:	2½ (U.S.) gallons. Finish as U.K. models. Amber reflectors fitted under the front tank mountings.
Engine unit:	9 : 1 pistons. Cylinder head incorporating 1 $\frac{3}{16}$ in diameter inlet port adaptors tapering to 1⅛ in diameter inlet ports in the head.
Gearbox:	Standard ratio.
	19 T G/box drive sprocket.
Carburetters:	30 mm Amal Concentric carburetters, type 930 fitted.
Air filters:	2 separate pancake air filters with cloth elements.
Wheels:	3.25 x 19 in diameter Dunlop ribbed front – West Coast
	3.50 x 19 in diameter Dunlop K70 Universal front – East Coast
	4.00 x 18 in diameter Dunlop K70 Universal rear
Mudguards:	New, longer, stainless steel, front and rear.
Front forks:	New crown and stem to suit 2½ gallon fuel tank. Chromed dome nut fitted in lieu of steering damper.
Mufflers:	Straight-through absorption sports type mufflers.
Ignition coils:	Siba 32000/1
Stop/tail light:	Lucas type 679 with alloy casting fitted with red reflectors on each side.
Electrical Equipment:	Headlight switch/ignition switch interconnected to allow head and parking lights only when the ignition is switched on.

121

Right side view of the US 1968 T120R illustrating the Hi-Fi Scarlet fuel tank and chromed mudguards

| Twinseat: | Black top, black piping, black sides, chrome plastic lower rim trim band. |

The twinseat strap was superseded by a chrome tubular safety rail bolted to the rear of the twinseat for the West Coast models at DU.75452, followed by the East Coast models after engine No. DU.77018.

1969 model: Unit construction T120 model Bonneville 120
Commencing engine No. DU.85904 to DU.90282 and JC.00101 onwards

Models: T120 Bonneville 120
T120R Bonneville T120R

Engine

The crankshaft halves, gearbox inner and outer covers, timing and primary covers were all changed to incorporate UNF threads. The cylinder head inlet and exhaust port adaptor threads were also altered to the new UNF as were most of the studs, plugs, screws and nuts. For the first time the new UNF threaded carburetter inlet adaptors were interchangeable with the U.S. models, being 1 ³⁄₁₆ in diameter inlet tapering to 1⅛ in diameter at the inlet port throat in the head. The cylinder head now had steel sleeves pressed into the inner holding down stud holes to prevent breakthrough during the inlet port profile machining and polishing.

The opportunity was also taken to increase the feed capacity of the oil pump, by fitting an increased diameter feed plunger into a new oil pump body. Coincidentally, the oil scavenge pipe in the crankcase was raised ⅝ in to increase the residual oil level (from DU.88714) in a further attempt to reduce camshaft wear problems. A new oil pressure release valve was fitted utilising UNF threads whilst an electrical oil pressure switch was now fitted to the timing cover.

1969 model home and general export T120 with re-designed front drum brake actuating mechanism, new style tank badges and windtone horns. The tank top parcel grid was no longer specified for all Triumph model markets and variants

A new heavier flywheel was fitted at NC.02256 in October 1968 to the previous crankshaft, after the commencement of the 1969 series production to apply a 'smoothing' of inertia to the crankshaft assembly whilst at the same time maintaining the identical overall balance factor. This had the effect of reducing the 'peakiness' of the engine vibration, whilst not affecting the resonance relationship between the engine and the frame itself.

New connecting rods were introduced at GC.23016, now fitted with connecting rod bolts and self lock nuts utilising UNF threads. Resulting from this new thread angle and form, the tightening torque was amended from 28 lbf to 22 lbf ft. To complete the flywheel and crankshaft assembly change for 1969 the new Hepolite pistons were produced with an even thicker section crown and specified a shorter, heavier cross-section gudgeon (wrist) pin.

The season commenced with a revised pushrod cover tube design developed to overcome once and for all the problem of pushrod cover tube oil leakage. These were no longer dependent on trapping the tube vertically between sealing rings, but relied upon Viton 'O' rings top and bottom, located into internal grooves at the lower end, maintaining a diametral oil tight sliding fit over the tappet guide blocks and seated against the upper shoulder, providing an oil tight fit in the cylinder head counterbore. At engine No. PD.32574, an additional lower silicone rubber compression sealing washer had to be reintroduced at the tappet guide block, in conjunction with an additional pressed-on sleeve on the lower end of the pushrod cover tube to restrain this washer in position. This squeezed the new silicone top sealing washer into the cylinder head spot faced recess, and effectively sealed the lower end (exactly as previously). The pushrod cover tube itself was identified by top end castellations to remove any weir effect and prevent any possibility of excessive oil build-up within the inlet and exhaust valve cavities.

By far the most important change affecting service reliability long after the warranty had been forgotten was the introduction of nitrided surface treatment camshafts. This occurred at DU.87105, and put a complete and permanent end to camshaft wear problems. Cam wheels with revised timing marks were fitted from JD.25965 onwards. The incorporation of UNF threads in the crankcase allowed the change to a left-hand tachometer gearbox thread eliminating once and for all the problems of slackening and fracturing tacho-gearbox drives.

In response the worldwide police pressures to combat organised and systematic theft of motorcycles, the new crankcase from DU.86965 also incorporated a raised pad onto which a multiple Triumph logo pattern was embossed. Onto this the legitimate engine number was stamped as 123

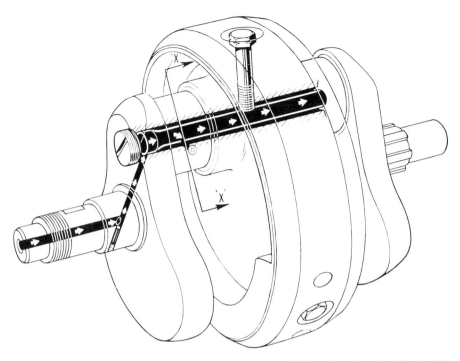

The heavy flywheel assembly replaced the narrow version which was introduced earlier in 1966, retaining the 85% balance factor

previously. Any attempt to deface or alter would henceforth immediately be visible and under X-ray technique, identifiable.

For 1969 the Amal type 930 Concentric carburetters dropped the replaceable pilot jets, incorporating a fixed internal calibrated drilling instead and changed the main jets from 210 to 190, and the needle jet from 0.107 to 0.106.

Gearbox

At the beginning of the season a new folding kick-start pedal (UNF bolt only) and a hexagonal UNF threaded camplate plunger spring housing nut accompanied a revision to the gearbox 3rd gear ratios. These were amended from 22/24 to 22/23 ratios from the commencement of the season. The 22 tooth layshaft gear from each combination, although similar, were neither identical in tooth form, or compatible in any way.

'Shaved' gears were introduced at the commencement of 1969, being of identical tooth form, but also being given a new range of part numbers. These new gears now incorporated an additional final tooth form shaving operation prior to heat treatment to ensure a better running surface finish thereby reducing surface wear and noise. To add to interchangeability problems, an improved camplate pressing, together with lengthened sleeve selector forks was incorporated mid season at DU.88630. But worse was to come!

Further major dimensional changes to the gearbox shaft running diameters, and gear pinion bore diameters were then introduced later in the season at engine No. CC.15546 with major interchangeability and potentially hazardous service problems should any of these come to be mixed with the previous gear and shaft combination.

Primary Chaincase

The only change to be introduced into the primary chaincase components, was that of a statically balanced clutch housing at engine No. DU.88383 to overcome any residual transmission vibration, identified by the deletion of the previous cast pockets.

Frame

There were no recorded changes for 1969.

Forks

To enable the fitting of bigger cross section tyres, the front fork stanchion tube centres were increased from 6½ to 6¾ inches. Additionally, two extra ⁵⁄₁₆ in diameter holes were added to the stanchions after AC.10464 to assist in the rebound damping control. Although the basic design and function remained the same, the top and bottom fork lugs were replaced to accomodate the fork leg centre dimensional change, important from the interchangeability and safety point of view, the front brake anchor plate lug peg on the right bottom sliding member was lengthened accordingly. A grommet in the headlamp mounting brackets and plastic clips were added to keep the control cables neater and tidier and a new chromed steering stem top nut was now fitted as standard, finally discontinuing fitment of the old standard Triumph steering damper equipment, available now only as additional equipment.

Fuel Tank

New style petrol tank badges required a new associated range of fuel tanks. These new badges were not dissimilar to the 1966/7/8 series, but the Triumph motif itself now became inset within a square 'picture frame' border. The tank centre styling strap was retained in position by means of a simple threaded hook. The previous year's oil tank continued, utilising a metered oil supply to the rear chain, controlled by a metering screw in the filler cap.

Rear Suspension

The new swinging arm was indentical to the previous year but manufactured in a heavier gauge material. The Girling oil controlled rear suspension now deleted the dust covers and incorporated external and visible chrome-plated springs providing the new sporty look for 1969.

Brakes

Front:	Full width 8 in diameter finned cast iron hub with twin leading shoe front brake incorporating an air screw in the front brake anchor plate.
Rear:	7 in diameter cast iron drum with bolt-on steel sprocket and a standard wheel, and integral teeth on the cast iron Q.D. wheel.

Fully floating shoes were fitted to the front and rear brakes. The front brake anchor plate was changed to allow fitment of a new front brake cam lever operated linkage with alternative vertical operating cable access, thereby eliminating the looped cable arrangement of the previous year.

Wheels

The front wheel with 3.00 x 19 in diameter Dunlop ribbed tyre now incorporated a longer spindle, alternative internal grease retainers and sported a new chromed cover plate. This featured concentric ribs in lieu of the previous fluting.

The rear wheel continued with a 3.50 x 18 in diameter Dunlop K70 Universal rear tyre equipment.

Mudguards

Painted steel front and rear mudguards were specified.

Exhaust System

With worldwide sound level legislation closing in on the manufacturer, and the sales climate demanding ever increasing performances, the next step on the precarious ladder of achievement of both ideals was the introduction of the coupled exhaust system. The first version for 1969 was rapidly followed by the second version utilising simpler balance pipe connections (to allow easier removal after extended service). The improvement in noise level achieved allowed the home and general export market to utilise as standard equipment the sports straight-through absorption type muffler equipment previously reserved for the U.S. market for the preceding three years.

Air Filters

All Bonneville model variants continued to use pancake type air filters, specifying for U.K. coarse paper elements.

Instruments

No change took place to the instrument equipment. The major change was the revised tachometer drive gearbox incorporating a left-hand threaded (UNF) securing screw to overcome loosening off in service.

Electrical Equipment

The new Lucas RM21 encapsulated stator now became standard production equipment, a major step forward in the provision of increased generator output. All Bonneville models now specified twin Winthorne horns (and associated horn relay equipment) as standard, but with a stronger mounting bracket (sic!) from DU.89530, and even louder horns from engine No. CC.14783. A new rear number plate pressing on U.K. models allowed fitment of the U.S. specification Lucas L679 rear stop/tail light.

For 1969 the new oil pressure switch acted within the ignition warning light circuit (i.e. it went out with the engine running . . . . unless of course an oil pressure failure caused it to re-illuminate, in which case it became advisable immediately to switch off the ignition and investigate – as the rider handbook for 1969 stated!) An electrical pressure sensitive switch incorporated in the front brake cable now acted as an additional rear stop lamp operating switch.

Twinseat

Another new twinseat! This time it was fully interchangeable with the previous range, but now it incorpoated threaded bolt holes in the base pan to allow fitment of a rear passenger tubular grab rail, and had in fact, been specified halfway through the 1968 season on U.S. models.

Finish

Frame:	Black
Forks:	Black
Mudguards:	Front – silver with Olympic Flame stripe, lined gold
	Rear – silver with Olympic Flame stripe, lined gold
Petrol tank:	Two-tone, Olympic Flame top/silver lower half with gold separating line
Oil tank:	Black
Toolbox cover:	Black

Extras

Quickly detachable rear wheel, and Overseas handlebars remained available as standard extras. Pillion footrests, prop stand and steering lock were included in the standard machine specification.

U.S. Alternatives

T120R Bonneville model (52 claimed bhp at 6,500 rpm).

Fuel tank:	2½ (U.S.) gallons. Finish as U.K. Models Amber side reflectors
Engine unit:	As U.K. models.
Gearbox:	Standard ratios. 19 T G/box sprocket.
Carburetters:	30 mm Amal type 930 Concentric carburetters.
Air filters:	Two separate pancake type with filter cloth and gauze elements.
Wheels:	3.25 x 19 in diameter Dunlop K70 Universal front 4.00 x 18 in diameter Dunlop K70 Universal rear.
Front forks:	Alternative crown and stem to allow smaller fork turning circle to suit 2½ U.S. gallon fuel tank.
Mufflers:	Straight-through absorption sports type mufflers.
Ignition coils:	Siba 32,000/1

Left side view of the 1969 USA model Bonneville supplied to both east and west Coasts. The fluted front brake drum cover was superseded by a chromed cover featuring four concentric ribs. The passenger grab rail was bolted to the underside of the twinseat pan

This right side photograph illustrates the new fuel tank badges, and the new rear suspension units introduced with the 1969 USA Bonneville models

Electrical equipment:

Headlamp switch/ignition switch connected to allow head and parking lights only with ignition switched on.

Red reflectors fitted to each side of tail lamp casting.

Handlebars:

Additional cups added to raise the mountings, together with associated steady rubbers and distance pieces to obviate possible fouling of the base of the eyebolts against the frame steering lock flange.

Right-hand view of the 1970 home and general export T120 Bonneville model showing the even larger windtone horns. The twinseat grab rail now became part of the rear lifting handle. The colour finish was Astral Red with Silver side panels. Mudguards were Astral Red with Silver stripe lined Gold

1970 Model: Unit construction T120 model Bonneville 120
Commencing Engine No. JD.24849
Models: T120 Bonneville 120
*   T120R Bonneville T120R*

Engine

Deletion of the previous Triumph style inlet camshaft operated timed engine breather system necessitated the introduction of a new drive side crankcase, which incorporated the latest service pre-sized camshaft bushes, requiring the new timing side crankcase to match. Engine breathing was now achieved by drilling three breather holes in the drive side crankcase below the main bearing housing, allowing pressure relief into the primary chaincase chamber, at the same time maintaining a constant residual oil level in the chaincase.

A new pair of camshafts were specified, nitrided as previously, but both introducing UNF threads and new camshaft nuts. The inlet cam discontinued the breather tube and slotted breather disc drive. The engine drive sprocket reverted to an earlier energy transfer pattern with its associated spacer, enabling conversion to competition ignition equipment with the minimum of disruption.

The Amal type 930 carburetters were finally converted to incorporate float bowls with plastic drain plugs, which although being a most desirable feature still did not, unfortunately, allow jet removable or replacement with the float bowl in situ.

Gearbox

Modification of the gearbox inner cover allowed fitment of a shorter selector rod (thereby eliminating a further potential oil leakage zone) and the specification of a heavier section main bearing circlip, eliminating any possibility of 'springing out' from engine No. AD.37473. Machines subsequent to ED.51080 now had aluminium bronze selector forks with integral rollers, but the major departure for 1970 was the changeover to a precision pressing camplate and leaf spring indexing at engine No. ED.52044.

Primary Transmission

The new engine breathing system required further modification within the primary chaincase, in the form of a breather cover plate inboard of the clutch, replacing the previous primary chaincase oil catchment trough and feed line, acting as a baffle plate and conecting to an external breather elbow pipe above the gearbox casting. The alternator cable outlet was also relocated to feed out the cable above the top of the gearbox casing. Occasional clutch thrust washer tab fracture resulted in the introduction of a revised clutch hub (less thrust washer location holes) and thrust washer less location tabs.

Frame

Bolt-on front engine plates fitted to cross-tubes welded into the front downtubes reduced initial engine assembly time and considerably aided engine removal for servicing, and the introduction of a prop stand with an adjustable stop were the only two frame modifications for 1970.

Forks

Although the 1970 Replacement Parts lists indicate a new set of forks for 1970 models, the only actual changes were that of two additional oil bleed holes in the stanchions introduced at AC.10464, and replacement of the earlier machined 'pommel' type front mudguard mounting lugs, by welded-on steel pressings and square nuts onto the sliding bottom outer members.

Left side view of the 1970 home and general export T120 Bonneville model, illustrating the new engine breather pipe routing down the left side of the rear mudguard

Fuel Tank

The fuel tank change was simply that of the new seasonal introduction, this year of Astral Red panels on a silver background, gold lined.

Oil Tank

A new oil tank of increased capacity (5½ pints Imperial – 6 pints U.S.) was fitted.

Rear Suspension

The Girling suspension units introduced new improved castellated load adjuster sleeves, designed to protect the adjusters from water and grit ingress.

Brakes

Brake specification was identical to the previous year, but a flat steel strip type rear brake anchor plate to swinging arm torque stay replaced the tabular pattern.

Wheels

The front wheel with 3.00 x 19 in diameter Dunlop K70 ribbed front tyre continued without change from the previous year, whereas the rear still specifying 3.50 x 18 in diameter K70 Universal tyre, with a changeover to UNF threaded rear hub, rear wheel brake drum and sprocket bolts, together with speedometer drive adaptor.

Mudguards

New front and rear painted steel mudguards, only varied in part number to signify the change in finish from the previous year. The rear guard, however, incorporated hole piercings to locate the new silvered finish ('D' section) plastic engine breather pipe routing. The rear lifting handle/mudguard stay was now additionally incorporating a looped rear passenger grab rail, replacing the bolt-on version introduced onto the twinseat the previous year.

Exhaust System

No change was introduced onto the U.K. and general export system, which incidentally, now became standard equipment on the U.S. version of the Bonnie.

Air Filters

Filter cloth and gauze element were specified for the twin pancake air filters, in line with previous U.S. models.

Electrical Equipment

The new smaller oil filled Lucas 17M 12 ignition coils were specified for 1970. A change in the headlamp bulbholders signified the only need to change the part number; in practice this was not a new lamp for 1970 models. Two additional sliding brackets were fitted to the Windtone horn mountings, to restrain their movement and avoid any possibility of contact with the front mudguard, at engine No. ED.44339.

Instruments

No change was recorded of instruments fitted to the Bonnie for 1970 models.

Twinseat

A new twinseat pan pressing allowed the seat to be lowered.

Finish

Frame:	Black
Forks:	Black
Mudguards:	Front – Astral red with silver stripe, lined gold
	Rear – Astral red with silver stripe, lined gold
Petrol tank:	Astral background with silver side panels, lined in gold
Oil tank:	Black
Toolbox cover:	Black

Extras

Quickly detachable rear wheel, and Overseas handlebars continued as available extra equipment. The prop stand, pillion footrests and steering lock were included in the standard machine equipment.

U.S. Alternatives (Claimed bhp 52 at 6,500 rpm).

Fuel tank:	2½ (U.S.) gallons, colour finish as U.K. but with swept-wing gold lined silver panels on the tank top. Amber reflectors fitted under the front fuel tank mountings.

The right side view of the 1970 T120R for the US market illustrates the swept wing Gold lined Silver panels on the Astral Red fuel tank and Astral Red painted fenders with Silver central stripe, lined Gold

The 1970 T120R viewed from the left side

Engine unit:	As U.K. models.
Gearbox:	As U.K. standard ratio.
	19 T G/box sprocket.
Carburetters:	As U.K. – Amal 930 Concentric type, 190 main jets.
Wheels:	3.25 x 19 in Dunlop K70 Universal front.
	4.00 x 18 in Dunlop K70 Universal rear.

Mudguards:	Chrome-plated mudguard stays, front and rear.
Front forks:	Alternative crown and stem to allow tighter fork turning circle to suit 2½ (U.S.) gallon fuel tank.
Mufflers:	As U.K.
Ignition coils:	As U.K.
Electrical Equipment:	Headlight switch/ignition switch connected to allow head and parking lights only with the ignition switched on.
	Red reflectors fitted to each side of the tail light casting.
Handlebars and control cables:	U.S. specification.

Late 1971 home T120R Bonneville fitted with the 4-gallon (Imp.) petrol tank in Tiger Gold and Black, still retaining the USA type high rise handlebars

197.1 model: Unit construction T120 model Bonneville 120
Commencing engine No. NE.01436
Models: T120 Bonneville 120
T120R Bonneville T120R

Engine

A new cylinder head, specifically machined to accept the new cylinder head bolts, and modified to accept the internally milled rocker boxes to allow assembly after engine fitted into the frame, also required the addition of four locating dowel pegs. The pushrod cover tube was amended to incorporate a full unbroken rim, deleting the castellations in favour of drain hole piercings, with the lower end perpetuating the 1969 season service fix silicone washer and sleeve.

The timing side crankcase was changed to incorporate a one-piece UNF threaded oil pressure relief valve. Although now of UNF thread, this unit comfortably fits all previous applications. Other engine unit changes were the fitment of a new flywheel, new flywheel bolts and flat washers onto the previous (since 1963) crankshaft. A new engine drive sprocket without the ground oil seal shoulder face and an associated modified distance piece to compensate for the fitting of primary chain alignment shims, was introduced to ensure more positive and accurate chain alignment. The drive side crankshaft oil seal was deleted.

Ensuing from a worldwide shortage of ball and roller bearings emergency action resulted in conversion of the timing side crankcase, and the crankshaft itself being modified to accept a metric timing side (R.H.) ball bearing at engine No. GE.27029.

Gearbox

No changes were made to the gearbox for 1971.

Primary Transmission

Late in the season (there is no recorded engine introduction number) the clutch shock absorber centre was drilled through, allowing the threaded outer plate to be retained by three hexagon headed through-bolts from the rear inner plate. The bolts were staked permanently into position.

Frame

An entirely new one-piece front/rear duplex (twin front downtube) frame, with central large diameter thin walled tabular spine additionally acted as the engine oil tank. New centre and prop stands, swinging arm and chain guard, left and right air cleaner assemblies, covers and side panels were introduced, together with an associated new range of footrests, engine mounting plate hardware and rear footbrake pedal.

Forks

The front forks also were entirely new both in detail design and hydraulic damping concept. Mounted on adjustable taper roller steering head frame bearings, the aluminium fork outer members were controlled by a new internal oil damper tube and valve assembly. Rubber bush mounted headlamp bracket in chrome-plated wire framework was featured, whilst the front wheel spindle was clamped with aluminium caps located by four studs and nuts at the base of each leg.

Fuel Tank

A new three gallon (Imp) petrol tank, rubber mounted with a single central fixing bolt was introduced with the new frame, complete with new chromed tank styling strips, but featuring the previous tank badges and petrol taps. Tank knee-grips were discontinued. A four (Imp) gallon petrol tank with flat sloping sides was fitted for the U.K. and general export markets later in the season.

Oil Tank

Now incorporated within the frame main tube of 4 pints (Imp) capacity, the oil feed to the engine being through an integral 'top hat' wire mesh oil filter and sump plate (later to be superseded by a separate sump filter and plate to aid servicing).

Rear Suspension

New rear suspension units with 110 lb rate chromed springs were fitted.

Brakes

A new 8 in twin leading shoe brake with massive air scoop, large brake shoes and Micam brake shoe adjusters accessible through the hub itself was the new feature. Later, an additional compression spring was introduced between the front brake anchor plate cam levers to ensure continual satisfactory seating of the front brake cable in the lever abutments. The rear brake fitted thicker liners in April 1971 after initial production, together with thicker fulcrum pads and the necessary longer rear brake cam lever (in conjunction with a newly introduced return spring to increase the leverage). The new, longer lever was installed 'upwards' instead of underslung as previously. There is no recorded engine number change point for either of these alterations to restore braking efficiency.

133

1971 Aluminium rear wheel hub and brake drum

Wheels
New alloy conical hubs were fitted to both wheels, the front fitting a 3.25 x 19 in diameter Dunlop K70 Universal tyre, and the rear specifying 4.00 x 18 in diameter Dunlop K70 Universal, 47 teeth rear wheel bolt-on sprocket, requiring a 106 link rear chain. The overall gear ratio was thus lowered once again, calling for greater engine rpm.

Mudguards
The new painted steel front mudguard, integral with its own stays, was clamped via rubber bushes to the aluminium fork sliding outer members. A black plastic number plate was fitted to U.K. and general export models.

Exhaust System
New exhaust pipe and silencers were specified utilising the previous exhaust pipe clips, stays and connector pipe.

Air Filters
Two large, readily accessible square wire mesh/filter cloth air filter elements were now housed in black plastic air cleaner assembly bodies and covers mounted either side of the frame under the twinseat, connected directly via rubber connector pipes to the carburetter intakes.

Electrical Equipment
A new flat 'pan' shaped, chromium-plated headlamp shell was now fitted incorporating three warning lights (ignition/oil – red, main beam – green, direction indicator – amber) and a two position rotary light switch. A 45/35 watt headlamp bulb instead of the previously developed anti-vibration 50/40 watt (446) to meet prevalent legislative requirements. A new Yale type ignition master switch was fitted to the right-hand side panel under the twinseat. A single Lucas (6H) horn replaced the previous Windtones. The most important feature however was the introduction of the new Lucas handlebar mounted integral switch consoles. The left incorporated a horn push, dip switch and headlamp main beam flashing button, whilst the right console carried the direction indicator switch and engine kill-button. A new plastic rear footbrake pedal operated stop lamp switch was screwed onto the rear frame member.

Instruments

New (1600 cable rpm) speedometer, rubber cup mounted, with matching (4 : 1) tachometer were fitted, the rubber cups ring mounted on brackets clamped under the two fork stanchion chromed cap nuts.

Twinseat

New, and hinged as previously to suit the new rear frame section, but now incorporating an external, but lockable seat catch assembly.

Finish

Frame:	Black
Forks:	Alloy sliders
	Chromed headlamp mounting brackets.
Mudguards:	Front – Tiger gold, black stripe, lined white.
	Rear – Tiger gold, black stripe, lined white.
Petrol tank:	Tiger gold with black 'swept-wing' scallop panel, lined white. Four gallon (Imp) fuel tank finished in Tiger gold with black central top stripe, lined white, and black horizontal lower band, lined white.

It was only later in the 1971 season the 4-gallon (Imp.) slab-sided home and general export petrol tank was specified whilst retaining the USA handlebar. This model had a Tiger Gold finish with a lower Black horizontal tank band, lined White, with a central tank top Black 'racing' stripe, also lined White

Air filter assemblies:	Black
Side panels:	Black, Gold (Bonneville).

U.S. Alternatives

Fuel tank:	3 gallon (U.S.) – (4¾ gallon U.S. available)
	Colour finish as U.K.
Engine unit:	As U.K.
Gearbox:	As U.K. (Standard ratio, 19 T G/box sprocket)
Carburetters:	As U.K.
Air filter:	Coarse filter elements.
Wheels:	As U.K.

135

The 1971 650cc model T120R supplied to home, export and the USA markets for the early part of the season with the 3-gallon (3.6 US) fuel tank with Black swept-wing scallop panels, lined White

Mudguards:	As U.K. but front guard less number plate mounting bolt hole piercings.
Ignition coils:	As U.K.
Electrical Equipment:	As U.K.
Handlebars and controls:	Twin rotor twist-grip with longer control cables.
Front forks:	As U.K.
Mufflers:	U.S. mufflers to suit legislative requirements.

1972 model: Unit construction T120 model Bonneville 120
Commencing engine No. HG.30870
Models: T120R Bonneville 120R
T120 RV Bonneville 120RV

Engine
The metric timing side ball bearing had been introduced in June 1971 immediately prior to the commencement of the 1972 season, affecting the timing side crankcase and crankshaft assembly. This continued for 1972 with the incorporation of new camshaft pinions deleting the central threaded extractor boss now replaced by two threaded extractor holes, and with a reversion to the earlier type

Left-hand view of the 1972 home and general export T120R model, still retaining the wire mounted pan-shaped headlamp shell unit, more readily indentified by the decorative "Bonneville" side panel decals introduced for 1972 models

composite oil pressure release valve at engine number CG50464. At XG.42304 a new cylinder head with exhaust ports designed to accept the new push-in exhaust pipes was fitted, which also specified bolt-on cast aluminium inlet port adaptors replacing the previous threaded variety. In order to simplify and aid in rocker adjustment a completely new inlet and exhaust rocker box with finned flat covers replaced the old type (x 4) inspection caps. Four new internal cylinder head holding down bolts and associated rocker box bolts were also required.

Gearbox
A new internal (3 ball) clutch lever was fitted to eliminate lost movement and to improve clutch action. Five-speed gears were offered as an alternative on RV models.

Frame
A new, lower frame, calling for an abbreviation of the height of the air filter assembly outer covers and side panels was now specified. Subsequent to engine No. CG.50414, a new electrical coil mounting plate incorporating a form of tool tray replaced the earlier pattern, providing greater electrical component separation and accessibility.

Forks
A new bottom yoke and stem assembly changed the top nut thread from 16 to 24 UNF whilst the new fork sliding outer members were not polished.

Fuel Tank
The 4 gallon (Imp) (4¾ U.S. gallons) – 'slab-sided' petrol tank was fitted to all U.K. and general export models offered as an alternative on U.S. models. Stick-on knee grips were introduced on the large tank.

Oil Tank
Of 4 pints (Imp) capacity continued to be incorporated within the frame main tube.

Rear Suspension Unit
Girling hydraulically damped rear suspension units were fitted, with external chromed springs.

Brakes
No change was made from the previous year's model.

Wheels
No change was made from last year's models.

Mudguards
The front mudguard was fitted with a reinforcing central stay assembly to provide three points of fixing per side to eliminate stay fracture.

Exhaust system
'Push-in' exhaust pipes were introduced at XB.42304 retaining the previous connector pipe, silencers, clips, brackets and stays.

Air Filters
No change was made from the previous year's model.

Electrical Equipment
In response to public demand and press criticism, the handlebar switch locations were reversed, to provide the horn push, dip switch and handlebar flasher button to the right, with the direction indicator switch and ignition kill button to the left. A new louder Lucas 6H horn was fitted whilst the indicator lamp stanchions were commonised with the T150 model.

Instruments
No change was made to the instrument equipment from the previous year's model.

Handlebars
Alternative specification (increased fulcrum radius) alloy brake and clutch levers were fitted in conjunction with their associated switch console lever half castings.

Twinseat
The new twinseat was padded and covered to assist in lowering the overall rider's seat height (now claimed to have returned to the original earlier Bonnie seat height of 31½ in).

Right side view of the 1972 home and general export model of the T120R. It will be noted the twinseat was amended, in conjunction with the lowered frame, in an attempt to reduce the overall height of the machine

Finish

Frame:	Black
Forks:	Alloy sliders
	Chromed headlamp mounting brackets
Mudguards:	Front – Tiger gold, Cold White centre stripe, lined black
	Rear – Tiger gold, Cold White centre stripe, lined black
Petrol tank:	Tiger gold, with Cold White horizontal (lower quarter) stripe, lined in black
Air filter assemblies:	Black
Side panels:	Black – gold decals.

The US version of the 1972 T120RV model fitted with the 3 (US)-gallon 'round' gasoline tank, finished in Tiger Gold top, with Cold White lower top and side panels, lined Black

U.S. Alternatives

Fuel tank:	3 gallon (U.S.) round tank. Finish Tiger Gold with Cold White scallop top and side panels, lined black. (Optional 4¾ U.S. gallon available) (as U.K.)
Engine unit:	As U.K.
Gearbox:	As U.K. (Five-speed standard)
Carburetters:	As U.K.
Air filters:	Coarse filter element.
Mudguards:	T120 – painted front and rear
Ignition coils:	As U.K.
Electrical equipment:	As U.K.
Handlebars and controls:	Twin rotor twist-grip.
Front forks:	As U.K.
Mufflers:	U.S. specification megaphone type (71-2382) mufflers.

The home model version of the 1973 750cc **T140V** Bonneville incorporating the front disc brake. Finished in Hi-Fi Vermillion with Gold scalloped side panels, lined White. The mudguards were chrome finish front and rear

1973 Model: Unit construction T120 model Bonneville 120
Commencing Engine No. JH.15366 – 650 model JH.15435 – 750cc model
Models: T120R   T120RV   T140V   T140RV

Engine

Production continued manufacturing the 1972 specification T120 models for 1973 but for the T140 models the engine was converted to 724cc (44 cu in) up to engine No. XH.22018. The bore/stroke ratio in this first series was 75 x 82 mm. From XH.22019 onwards the bore/stroke ratio was amended to 76 x 82 mm, giving a capacity of 747cc (45 cu in). Apart from the piston/cylinder barrel combination for each series, the newly introduced components remained substantially common for both models. New crankcases to accommodate the bigger cylinder barrel were introduced with the associated new crankshaft assembly (but last year's flywheel) new heavier section connecting rods and new flywheel bolts. A heavier duty metric timing side bearing was fitted.

Revised inlet and exhaust camshafts were now specified in conjunction with ¾ in radius inlet cam followers (tappets) and 1⅛ in diameter timed (oil feed) exhaust tappets.

A new 750cc cylinder head (incorporating an additional central fixing now in the form of two 5/16 in studs to aid assembly) together with an amendment to the cylinder head allowed the addition of locating dowels between the head and rocker boxes (to eliminate any movement and protect the gaskets). Also specified were the new cast aluminium inlet port adaptors (1⅛ in inlet port diameter) and a new manifold balance pipe, new inlet and exhaust valve guides and bottom spring cups, pushrods and pushrod cover tubes.

The increased power available required the use of a ⅜ in pitch triplex primary drive chain, with associated engine shaft drive sprocket.

The increased induction breathing rate continued to utilise the previous 30 mm diameter choke sized Amal type 930 Concentric carburetters, requiring only a main jet size change to 210.

Gearbox

The five-speed gearbox became standard equipment on the 750cc model, requiring a 20 tooth gearbox drive sprocket. A new high gear assembly was introduced for 1973 750cc model, together with a new layshaft assembly introducing a circlip location of the high gear pinion in preference to a pressed-on shoulder location.

Late 1973 models also suffered an irritating problem of jumping out of gear, and in consequence a gear conversion had been introduced which was incorporated as standard. This pack comprised mainshaft first and second gears, layshaft first, second and third gears, layshaft first gear selector fork and the layshaft first gear driving dog. At the same time a further mid-season improvement was the incorporation of the T150 gearchange operating camplate and indexing plunger.

Primary Transmission
The ⅜ in pitch triplex primary chain required a new triplex clutch housing, with 30% stronger clutch springs being incorporated to carry the increased torque loadings. Additionally, a new clutch shock absorber spider unit was also fitted.

Frame
A new frame assembly was introduced for the T140 series of models, the side covers deleting the moulded 'flutes' and the right side panel deleting the ignition switch piercing. The original type of Triumph hinged seat plunger/catch combination was incorporated together with a different engine cylinder head torque steady for the T140 engine unit. The front fairing tubular mounting lugs were deleted from the steering head pressing.

Forks
Rubber gaiters and chromed fork top outer covers were introduced, into which were mounted the new black painted headlamp brackets, the left-hand of which incorporated the ignition/master switch. New top and bottom fork yokes, the top having additional slots to allow clamping of the stanchion top spigots by means of hexagon headed cap screws. The top lug also incorporated a boss to accommodate the upper hydraulic pipe junction with the hydraulic front brake master cylinder hose.

The fork sliding members and stanchions were interchangeable with those of the T150 model at the introduction of the disc brake and caliper assembly. A new fork spring was specified but was interchangeable with the previous version, dimension/stroke differences being accommodated in the new spring top abutment threaded cap screw, onto which was mounted the chromed instrument brackets, being retained by an additional top cap nut, located into the new threaded cap screw. The internal hydraulic damper tube and valve assembly utilised for the previous two years continued in use.

Fuel Tank
The 4 gallon (Imp) 'slab-sided' petrol tank continued on the home and general export market.

Oil Tank
The frame capacity still continued at 4 pints (Imp, 4.8 U.S.) but to overcome doubt cast by varying claimed figures in official publications, a dipstick was incorporated integral with the frame oil tank filler cap.

Rear Suspension
Shorter units were fitted as part of the exercise to lower the seat height of the machine (by ½ in) with a loss of only 0.2 inches in movement.

Brakes
The major feature for 1973 was of course the appearance of the new disc front brake, with master cylinder on the right handlebar, and the front wheel disc and caliper on the left side. The rear wheel 7 in diameter single leading shoe brake continued unchanged.

Wheels
The front wheel hub was modified to incorporate the new 10 in diameter disc. A 3.25 x 19 in diameter K70 Universal front tyre was fitted. The rear wheel continued unchanged.

Mudguards
The new steel front and rear mudguards were chromium-plated.

Left view of the 1973 home and general export model T140V with US type megaphone silencers and front number plate

Exhaust System
New, quieter, longer slimline silencers were fitted, in conjunction with the associated new exhaust pipes fitted to U.K. models, and were identified by the pronounced curved-tapered end cones (71-3723).

Air Filters
New air cleaner bodies (left and right-hand) covers and elements were fitted. The right-hand panel no longer incorporated the ignition/master switch piercing, and the side covers deleted the previous fluting.

Electrical Equipment
The latest Lucas 10CA contact breaker and auto advance unit was fitted. The pan-shaped headlamp shell was dropped in favour of the earlier pattern tear-drop style, with the (S.45) Yale key type ignition/master switch in the left hand fork cover, (as 1966/70) and a new 3 position (57SA) toggle switch in the headlamp shell. A completely new stop/tail light assembly meeting the latest U.S. Federal lighting requirements (Lucas L917) was fitted in conjunction with a new aluminium alloy rear mounting assembly.

Handlebars
New handlebars were fitted (8 in rise) to accommodate the new hydraulic front brake master cylinder.

Twinseat
A new twinseat, reverting to the earlier Triumph type seat catch and locating plunger was introduced. The seat profile was also changed to discontinue the rear tip-up effect, in place of a softer rounded rear end, effectively lowering the seat height and increasing the seat area.

Finish

Frame:	Black
Forks:	Black top outer covers
	Black headlamp brackets
	Polished alloy sliders and black rubber gaiters
Mudguards:	Front – chrome-plated steel
	Rear – chrome-plated steel
	chromed braces and rear lifting handle

The 1973 US version of the T140, with chromed fenders, 2½ (US)-gallon gasoline tank in Hi-Fi Vermillion paint finish, Gold upper scallops, lined White, front disc brake, and return to the more traditional Triumph front fender, fork and headlamp features

Petrol tank: Hi-Fi vermillion with gold scalloped side panels,
                                lined white
Air filter assemblies: Black
Side panels: Black, screw-on model identification badges
                                (silver lettering on red ground)

U.S. Alternatives
Fuel tank: New slimline 2½ gallon (U.S.) gas tank. Hi-Fi
                                vermillion with gold upper scallops, white pin
                                striping.
Wheels: 4.00 x 18 in diameter K81 Universal rear tyre
                                fitted.
Handlebars: Twin rotor twist-grip.
Forks: Chromed top outer covers.
                                Black headlamp brackets.
                                Less fork gaiters.
Mufflers: U.S. specification megaphone type (71-2382)
                                mufflers continued to be fitted on U.S. export
                                models.

The 1974/5 5-Speed 650cc Bonneville T120V model in home and general market trim. The colour scheme was Purple petrol tank with Cold White side panels, Gold lined, with chromed mudguards

1974 Model: Unit construction T140 model Bonneville T140
Commencing engine No. GJ.55101
Models: T120V Bonneville T120 T120RV Bonneville T120
T140V Bonneville T140 T140RV Bonneville T140

Engine

T120 models continued to be completed, but the emphasis was now turning to production of the larger T140 model. The new rocker boxes with finned flat covers introduced on 1973 T120 and T140 models were superseded by rocker boxes of amended design, each incorporating two extra cover fixing set screws, together with improved and modified gaskets to provide better sealing.

The new 75/85 lb oil pressure release valve varied in detail from the previous only in the incorporation of finer mesh filter gauze, all other comprising parts remaining common. The new nylon loaded oil pressure indicator switch, complete with associated extended rubber cover, was the only other visual change, other than the black plastic breather junction block outlet stub on the primary chaincase rear face. A new oil pump joint washer eliminating possible flow restrictions was also fitted.

Gearbox

The new layshaft assembly introducing circlip location of the high gear pinion in preference to the previous pressed-on shoulder location continued to be specified and fitted on 1974 models, together with an amended final drive sprocket, the outer face chamfered to suit the new sprocket nut lockwasher and oil sealing 'O' ring (to overcome oil seepage at the spline).

Frame

No changes were recorded between 1973 and 1974 models.

Forks

The steering damper was no longer offered as an alternative fitment. Chrome top fork covers continued, with rubber gaiters and black painted headlamp brackets remaining standard equipment for U.K. and general export markets.

Home market 750cc T140 1974/5 model Bonneville T140V finished in Red with Cold White side panels, Gold lined, with chromed mudguards

Fuel Tank
The four gallon (Imp) U.K. and general export petrol tank remained available with stick-on knee grips.

Rear Suspension
No changes were incorporated in the 1974 Girling rear suspension units from the previous 1973 season.

Brakes
A new rear brake cam and associated lever, again reversed, and fitted downwards was listed. (Although fitted halfway through the 1973 season, it was introduced to provide a strong tapered squared fit onto the brake camshaft, in lieu of the previous round shaft incorporating two 'flats' only. The new brake camshaft assembly was identified by an annular groove).

Wheels
Both front and rear wheels continued unamended from the previous season.

Mudguards
The front mudguard was attached to a thicker section fork leg mounting bracket.

Exhaust System
The new lower decibel silencers, identified by their reverse cone outlet and straight-sided tapering and section shape (replacing the previous U.K. and general export shell-shaped taper curved cone tail end section) were again developed to meet ever increasing sound level requirements.

Air Filters
The air filter elements and side panels continued from 1973 into 1974.

Electrical Equipment
No change was made to the electrical equipment specified for 1974.

Instruments
The previous year's speedometer and tachometer equipment continued for the 1974 season's models.

Handlebars
Last year's handlebars continued to be specified for the new season.

Twinseat
No change was made for 1974 models.

Finish

Frame:	Black
Forks:	Black top outer covers
	Black headlamp brackets
	Polished alloy sliders, black rubber gaiters
Mudguards:	Front – Chrome-plated steel) Chromed braces
	Rear – Chrome-plated steel) and rear lifting handle
Petrol tank:	T120 – Purple with Cold White side panels – gold lining
	T140 – Cherokee red with Cold White side panels with gold lining.
Air filter assembly:	Black
Side panels:	Black, with screw-on model identification badges (gold lettering on black ground)

U.S. Alternatives

Fuel tank:	3.6 (U.S.) gallon gas tank. T120 – Purple, Cold White tank top scallops, lined gold

The home version of the US variant of the 1974/5 5-Speed 650cc Bonneville T120RV model. The US 3½-gallon fuel tank was finished in Purple with Cold White tank top scallop panels, lined in Gold. Fenders were chromed. Fork covers were painted Black and the machine was fitted with rubber gaiters for the UK and general export markets UK silencers were also specified.

The home version of the 1974 US variant of the 1974/5 Bonneville T140RV. The colour finish was in Red with Cold White tank top scallop panels, lined in Gold with chromed fenders. The fork covers were painted Black for the UK and general export markets and rubber fork gaiters were fitted. UK silencers were fitted in lieu of the US megaphone type mufflers

	T140 – Cherokee red, Cold White tank top scallops, lined gold.
Handlebars:	U.S. specification 'high-rise' handlebars and control cables.
Front forks:	Chromed top outer covers, black headlamp brackets – no gaiters.

(Note: U.S. specification models released for the home and general export markets were fitted with chromed fork top outer covers, black headlamp brackets and fork gaiters.)

Historical Note

The last machine to be completed prior to the formation of the co-operative from existing stock parts was NJ.60083 in October 1973 (a 1974 model). The first machine to be entirely manufactured by the co-operative was a 1975 T140 model, engine No. DK.61000 on the 9th April 1975.

The first 1974 model Bonnies released between July and November 1974 from Meriden, following the factory blockade commencing in September 1973, were in the engine series numbers:

1974 T120 series models JJ.58080 to KJ.59067
1974 T140 series models KJ.59160 to NJ.60032

until the blockade was re-imposed on the 24th November 1974.

The balance of 1974 model production recommenced on 10th March 1975 (and continued to May 1975) engine numbers being as listed:

1974 T120 series models up to NJ.60070
1974 T140 series models up to EK.62239

1975 Model: Unit construction T140 model Bonneville T140
Commencing engine No. DK.61000

In March 1975, the co-operative recommenced assembly operations, completing the residual stock of unfinished 1974 models. On the 9th April, the first wholly manufactured machine by the co-operative (engine No. DK.61000) was completed and made ready for delivery as the first of the 1975 series production models.

Just over two months later, on 25th June that year, the last machine with the traditional right footshift (right foot-operated gearchange lever) was completed at engine No. GK.62239, and the first 1976 model with cross-over shaft left-side footshift, complete with the new rear disc brake assembly was introduced on production on 10th July.

The 1975 series production models were therefore to be regarded as an extension of the previous 1974 range of models, and were of indentical specification.

Finish

Frame:	Black
Forks:	Black top outer covers
	Black headlamp brackets
	Polished alloy sliders
Petrol tank:	T120 – Purple with Cold White side panels, gold lining
	T140 – Cherokee red with Cold White side panels, gold lining
Air filter assembly:	Black
Side panels:	Black – with screw-on model identification badges (gold lettering on black background)

U.S. Model
As 1974 U.K. model

1976/77 home and general export model T140V illustrating the left foot shift and rear disc brake

1976 and 1977 Models: Unit construction T140 model Bonneville T140
1976 models commencing engine No. HN.62501
1977 models commencing engine No. GP.75000
Models: T140V Bonneville 140
    T140V Bonneville 140 Jubilee model

The opportunity was taken in 1977, the 25th Jubilee year of the reign of Queen Elizabeth II, to create a commemorative model as a strictly limited edition of exactly 1,000 machines suitably finished in Red, White and Blue for the U.K. Market and a strictly similar quantity for the U.S.A.

Each model was supplied complete with its own individual certificate of origin.

A further international edition of 400 models only were made against a very strong demand from Canada, Australia and New Zealand and some were eventually released to distributors in Europe.

Engine

In addition to the basic changes introduced for left foot shift operation for the 1976 models, the opportunity was taken to incorporate further design and production improvements.

A new cylinder block was fitted, being fully interchangeable in service, but utilising UNF cylinder head stud threads and requiring only two grades (low and high) of piston size on production assembly, in lieu of the previous three (low, medium and high) grades. The washers were also deleted from beneath the cylinder base fixing nuts.

The Amal carburetters both had late part numbers indicating Spanish type extended float

149

ticklers, and changes to the fuel feed banjo fibre washers.

Although the 8.6 : 1 compression ratio pistons continued to be available, a new 7.9 : 1 version was made available and fitted as standard to all models.

'O' rings were incorporated on the ignition timing hole plug and the oil pressure release valve, with revisions to the oil pipe junction block, feed and return pipes, and as a mid-season change, longer primary chaincase breather outlet stub fixing screws.

Gearbox

The major change was to left foot operation, necessitating new gearbox inner and outer covers and joint washers, to accommodate the associated left-foot shift gearchange spindle, spindle bush, gearchange operating quadrant, and kick-start axle.

Primary Transmission

The new gearchange operating cross-over shaft between the rear of the gearbox inner cover and the left foot shift pedal, passed through the central section of the two crankcase halves, to the rear of the crankshaft assembly and, operating via a 'stirrup', around the clutch assembly in the primary chaincase, and through the new primary chaincase outer cover. The new cover deleting the once familiar rotor inspection and timing cover, in favour of a screwed inspection plug and fixed pointer assembly.

Frame

The new left foot shift, rear disc brake design dictated the incorporation of a new frame assembly and associated rear swinging arm fork, to accept the new rear brake caliper and mounting plate assembly. Previously left and right-handed rider footrests were replaced by a common footrest unit, whereas the pillion footrests were replaced by modified left and right-handed equivalents which were angled 45° rearwards to comply with U.S. regulations. Changes were also made to the coil mounting platform and battery carrier assembly to allow clearance for assembly of the rear brake master cylinder.

Forks

No changes were made to the front forks for 1976 and 1977.

Fuel Tank

New petrol taps (Petcocks) were introduced, indicating on/off, reserve, to meet legislative requirements in U.S.A.

Oil Tank

The spine-frame oil tank capacity remained at 4 pints Imp. (4.8 U.S.)

Rear Suspension

No change was made to the Girling rear suspension units for the 1976/7 season.

Wheels

An entirely new rear wheel with disc brake was introduced for 1976. 3.25 x 19 in Dunlop K70 Universal front and 4.00 x 18 in Dunlop K70 Universal rear tyres continued to be specified and fitted.

Brakes

The previous disc brake front wheel continued with slight modifications to the disc thickness in order to standardize with the newly introduced disc rear brake (0.250 in to 0.235 in).

Mudguards

A new chromed front mudguard blade deleting the front number plate mounting holes and eliminating the centre and front stays in favour of the T160 model central bridge piece was introduced mid-season. A new chromed rear mudguard was also fitted.

Exhaust System

The two exhaust pipes and cross tube assembly continued, but the silencers were now fitted with an almost parallel tail end section, identified by the pronounced concave dished end plates. Left and right-handed brackets were needed to allow the new silencers (mufflers) to clear the rear disc brake hose.

Air Filters
The air filter plastic covers were now bolted from the outside, the filter elements being pierced to accommodate the new intake silencer tubes.

Electrical Equipment
New Lucas handlebar console control switches were fitted to both left and right handlebars. A new clutch operating lever assembly was required on the left side and a revised specification stop/tail lamp and direction indicators were fitted, the differences being of lens and construction only and remained fully interchangeable.

Handlebars
New handlebars incorporating revised knurling were specified for 1976 for both Home and Overseas models, to accommodate and locate the new handlebar electrical console control switches.

New Smiths speedometer and tachometer instruments were specified, deleting the previous N.V.T. 'wiggly-worm' motif on the face.

Twinseat
Slight variation of the seat pan allowed standardization of the front and rear twinseat seat hinges.

Finish

Frame:	Black
Forks:	Chromed fork covers
	Black headlamp brackets
	Polished alloy sliders
Mudguards:	Front – Chrome-plate steel – chrome lower brace
	Rear – Chrome-plated steel – chrome lifting handle
Petrol tank:	Poly-red
	Blue
Air filter assembly:	Black
Side panels:	Black, with screw-on motif identification badges (gold lettering on black ground)

U.S. Alternatives

Fuel tank:	3.6 (U.S.) gallons gas tank, Poly-red.
Handlebars:	U.S. specification 'high-rise' handlebars and associated longer control cables.
Front forks:	Chromed top outer covers, black headlamp brackets – (no fork gaiters).
Mudguards:	Chromed finish

Jubilee Models

Frame:	Black
Forks:	Chromed top outer covers
	Black headlamp brackets
	Polished alloy sliders
Mudguards:	Front: silver, blue stripe centre, red (outer) and white (inner) lined
	Rear: silver, blue centre stripe, red (outer) and white (inner) lined
Rear chainguard:	silver with blue styling stripe lined white (inner) and red (outer)
Petrol tank:	Home – silver with blue side panel, line white (narrow – inner), red (broad) and white (narrow –

The US version of the 1976/77 T140V, now with left foot shift and rear disc brake

The home version of the Jubilee Bonneville limited edition model – "One of a Thousand"

	outer) pin-stripe border.
	U.S.A. – silver with blue scallop panels, line white (narrow – inner), red (broad) and white (narrow – outer)
Side panels:	silver, with commemorative Jubilee badges
Twinseat:	Powder blue top and sides styled cover, with red piping and chromed lower rim trim band
Wheels:	Chromed rims, centre stripe blue, lined white (inner) and red (outer)
Tyres:	Dunlop K91 4.10 x 19 in (Front). Red Arrow 4.10 x 18 in (Rear)

In addition, the engine timing cover, the gearbox outer and primary chaincase cover and the tail lamp casting, were heavily chrome-plated.

Illustration of the 1978 home model T140 in Tawny Brown and Gold livery

1978 Model: Unit construction T140 model Bonneville 140
Commencing engine No. HX.00100
Models: T140V Bonneville T140 T140E Bonneville T140

Engine
The basic 76 mm bore and 82 mm stroke continued, maintaining the overall engine capacity of 744cc. Only very minor changes were made for the new season, which included 7.9 compression ratio pistons now standardised for all markets, and the introduction of the new 'eyeleted' composition material cylinder head gasket, replacing the previous troublesome copper version. Crankcases were now only supplied in pairs, and (from engine No. 02690 onwards) the rockers and adjusters were amended to UNF threads. The only other practical change was the introduction of a serrated lockwasher to locate the rotor/crankshaft nut.

Gearbox
The mainshaft high gear now became available as a separate replacement spare part without requiring the purchase of the associated roller bearing, and a gasket was introduced between the gearbox inner and outer covers.

Frame
The frame remained unchanged for 1978, the only slight difference being to the anchor bolt section of the pillion footrests, resulting in their becoming left and right-handed.

Forks
The black fork top outer covers for the U.K. and general export markets were discontinued in favour of the chromed versions used previously as standard on all U.S. machines. The most important change however was the introduction of the 'self-aligning' fork oil seal and retainer (97-7010) particularly in view of its success and interchangeability with previous versions.

Fuel Tank
The two fuel tanks 4 gallons (Imp) and 3.6 gallons (U.S.) continued to remain available.

Oil Tank
Of 4 pints (Imp) capacity, continued to be incorporated within the frame main tube.

Rear Suspension
Girling hydraulically damped rear suspension units were fitted to home and general export machines at the commencement of the season, but were replaced by the new Girling 'gas-shocks' being fitted to the U.S. models as standard later in the model year.

Brakes
No changes were made from the previous year's model.

Wheels
The front wheels now incorporated sealed wheel bearings, whilst the rear wheel now specified a new wheel rim, complete with 9 gauge spokes and associated spoke nipples.

Mudguards
Nylon interposing washers were introduced to the front and rear mudguard fixing bolts to protect the paint and chrome finishes, and the tail light carrier, previously black for the U.K. and chromed for the U.S. market, now became polished and lacquered alloy.

Exhaust System
No change was made to the 1978 exhaust system from the previous season's models.

Air Filters
The previous season's air filter elements continued. A slight amendment, with the introduction of the cover fixing bolt Location circlip to aid assembly was made, but the most important change was the introduction of plastic spring retained, decorative side panel styling covers.

Electrical Equipment
The most important change to the electrical system was the incorporation of a new headlight which now specified a quartz iodine (halogen) headlamp bulb, and necessitated a revised light unit and bulb holder. An alternative Lucas (6H) horn was now fitted, and later in the season, the Lucas PUZ5A battery was replaced by the Yuasa 12N9-4B-1 equivalent model.

Instruments
No change was made to the basic specification of the Smith's speedometer and tachometer, but alternative Veglia instruments were fitted to some model batches in order to maintain production and overcome supply difficulties. A modification was made to the driven gear thrust washer in the tacho drive gearbox to overcome possible drive fracture.

Handlebars
No change was made to the handlebar equipment for 1978, but the dual rotor twist-grip was discontinued for machines with the 'high-rise' handlebars in favour of a single rotor twist-grip and junction box throttle cable.

Twinseat
An entirely re-styled twinseat was fitted for 1978, in two colours, and in two versions. The seats were available in black vinyl with black piping, or brown vinyl with brown piping, specifying either narrow or wide nose section, to match the wide U.K. (4 gallons) or narrow (3.6 gallons U.S.) American fuel tank.

Finish
Frame:	Black
Forks:	Chromed top outer covers

	Black headlamp brackets
	Polished alloy fork sliders, black rubber gaiters
Mudguards:	Front – Painted, plain colour with curved thumb-nail flash on front sections
	Rear – Painted, plain colour with a wide styling band across guard below rear lifting handle tube
Petrol tank:	Painted, with side panels
Side panels:	Painted. with hockey-stick side flash. Screw-on identification badges – (gold lettering on white background) on Aquamarine and Candy Apple finishes, and black lettering on silver ground on Tawny brown finishes.
Colours available (Home models):	
Tawny brown and gold:	Polychromatic Tawny brown mudguards and petrol tank and brown seat. Front and rear guards were plain polychromatic Tawny brown, had gold styling bands across the blades, lined brown (narrow, inner) and white outer. The petrol tank had gold side panels, lined in brown (narrow, inner) and white outer line.
	Side styling panels were Tawny brown with gold hockey-stick stripe, lined brown inner and white outer.
Aquamarine and silver:	Polychromatic Aquamarine mudguards and petrol tank and black seat. Front and rear guards had silver styling bands across the blades, lined black (inner) gold (outer). Side styling panels, silver with Aquamarine hockey-stick stripe, lined black (inner) and gold (outer).

U.S. Alternatives

Fuel tank:	3.6 (U.S.) gallon gas tank, painted with upper scallops, and pin striping.
Handlebars:	U.S. specification 'high-rise' handlebars and associated longer control cables. Twin rotor twist-grip discontinued.
Front forks:	No fork gaiters.
Mudguards:	Chrome finish.

T140E Model

The T140E model was introduced on January 1st 1978, fitted with Amal Concentric Mk. II carburetters, and revised engine breather system, to comply with U.S.A. Federal legislation (Environmental Protection Agency) concerning regulations governing exhaust emission pollutant control. These changes required modifications to the air boxes and side panels.

Colours available:	(U.S. and general export models)
Tawny brown and gold:	Polychromatic Tawny brown fuel tank, with gold upper scallops lined brown (narrow, inner) and white (outer). Tawny brown seat and side panels in Tawny brown with a screw-on T140 Bonneville 750 motif in gold lettering and black ground.
Astral blue and silver:	Polychromatic Astral blue fuel tank, with silver upper scallops, with gold pin striping. Black seat with black side panels and screw-on T140 Bonneville 750 motif in gold lettering and black ground.

155

The 1978 T140 variant supplied to the US market in Black and Candy Apple Red, with chromed front and rear fenders

Black and Candy Apple red:

Black fuel tank, with Candy Apple red upper scallops, lined gold. Black seat with black side panels and screw-on T140 Bonneville 750 motif in gold lettering and black ground.

The black and Candy Apple red version of the 1978 U.S. model was also made available for the U.K. and other export markets, and was then fitted with rubber front fork gaiters and appropriate lighting equipment.

The 1978 Catalogue for the U.S.A. stated quite simply:

'The legend lives on'.

Appendix

Technical data & major part numbers year-by-year

MODEL YEAR	1959	1960	1961	1962	1963	1964	1965	1966	19
COMMENCING ENGINE NUMBER	020076	029364 to 020424 and D101 onwards	D7727	D15789	DU101	DU5825	DU13375	DU24875	DU
ENGINE									
BORE / STROKE M.M.	71 × 82	71 × 82	71 × 82	71 × 82	71 × 82	71 × 82	71 × 82	71 × 82	
CAPACITY C.C.	649	649	649	649	649	649	649	649	
CLAIMED B.H.P @ R.P.M. UK / US	46 @ 6.500	46 @ 6500	46 @ 6500	46 @ 6500	46 @ 6.500	47 @ 6700	50 @ 6.500 47 @ 6.700	47 @ 6.700 50 @ 6.500	47 50
CYLINDER HEAD (C/w guides and valve ports)	E4019	E4019	E4019	E4019	E4928	E5348 ES727(T)	E5348 ES727(T.T)	E5348 ES727(TT)	ES
INLET PORT DIAMETER (INS) U.K.									
INLET PORT DIAMETER (INS) U.S.A.									
INLET PORT ADAPTOR Diam (INS) U.K	E3940	E3940	E3940	E3940	E3940	E5349 E5350	E5349 E5350	E5349 E5350	E5
INLET PORT ADAPTOR Diam (INS) U.S.A.	E3940	E3940	E3940	E3940	E3940	E5351 E5352	E5351 E5352	E5351 E5352	
EXHAUST PORT ADAPTOR	E3583	E3583	E3583	E3583	E3583	E3583	E3583	E5914	E
VALVE ~ INLET (HEAD DIAM × INS)	E3310 (1½)	E3310 (1½)	E3310 (1½)	E3310 (1½)	E3310 (1½)	E4603 (1⁹⁄₃₂)	E4603 (1⁹⁄₃₂)	E4603 (1⁹⁄₃₂)	E4
VALVE ~ EXHAUST (HEAD DIAM × INS)	E3927 (1¹¹⁄₃₂)	E3927 (1¹¹⁄₃₂)	E3927 (1¹¹⁄₃₂)	E3927 (1¹¹⁄₃₂)	E3927 (1¹¹⁄₃₂)	E2904 (1⁷⁄₁₆)	E2904 (1⁷⁄₁₆)	E2904 (1⁷⁄₁₆)	E29
VALVE GUIDE ~ INLET	E3827	E3827	E3827	E3827	E3827	E3827	E3827	E3827	
VALVE GUIDE ~ EXHAUST	E3828	E3828	E3828	E3828	E3828	E3828	E3828	E3828	
VALVE SPRING ~ INNER	E3001	E3001	E3001	E3001	E3001	E3001	E3001 WHITE SPOT → RED GREY	E4221	
VALVE SPRING ~ OUTER	E3002	E3002	E3002	E3002	E3002	E3002	E3002 WHITE SPOT → RED GREY	E4222	
VALVE SPRING BOTTOM CUP	E1544	E1544	E1544	E1544	E1544	E1544	E1544	E6439	
CYLINDER BLOCK	E3332	E3332	E3332	E3332	E4546	E4546	E4546	E6304	
PISTON	CP157 (E3610)	CP157 (E3610)	CP157 (E3610)	CP157 (E3610)	CP157 (E3610)	CP200 (E5329)/UK-8.5:1 CP200 (E5329)T-11:1	CP206 (E6341) T-9:1 CP206 (E5819)T-11:1	CP206 (E6341) T-9:1 CP206 (E6343)T-11:1	E68
PISTON COMPRESSION RATIO	8.5:1	8.5:1	9.5:1	8.5:1	8.5:1	E5329-8.5:1 E5317-11:1	E5341-9:1 E5819-11:1	E63 E68	
PUSH RODS (ALLOY)	E2620	E2620	E2620	E2620	E2620	E2620	E2620	E2620	E
PUSH ROD COVER TUBE	E3646	E3646	E3646	E3646	E3646	E3646	E3646	E6000	E
PUSH ROD COVER TUBE BOTTOM CUP	E1544	E1544	E1544	E1544	E1544	E1544	E1544	E4746	
CRANKCASE ~ DRIVE SIDE (L/H)	E2892	E2892	E2892	E2892	E4534	E4534	E4534	E6303	
~ TIMING SIDE (R/H)	E3282	E2314	E2314	E2314	E4533	E4533	E5871	E5871	
MAIN BEARING D/S (L/H)	E1591	E1591	E1591	E1591	E1591	E1591 LOCATED D/S	BALL → ROLLER E1591 LOCATED D/S	E2879 LOCATED D/S	
MAIN BEARING T/S (R/H)	E1591	E1591	E1591	E1591	E1591	E1591	E1591	E1591	
CAMWHEELS	E1486R	E1486A	E1486A	E1496R	E4562	E4562	E4562	E4562	
No OF KEYWAYS	1	1	1	3	3	3	3	3	
TIMING PINION	E1472	E1472	E1472	E1472	E4564	E4564	E5447	E4564	
INTERMEDIATE PINION	E1471	E1471	E1471	E1471	E4566	E4566	E4566	E6159	
CRANKSHAFT	E3894	E3894	E3894	E3894	E4643	E4643	E4643	E4643	
FLYWHEEL	E3906	E3906	E3906	E4479	E4479	E4479	E5783	E6327	
FLYWHEEL BOLTS	E3907	E3907	E3907	E3907	E3907	E3907	E3907	E6328	
BALANCE FACTOR	50%	50%	50%	71%	85%	85%	85%	85%	
BALANCE WEIGHT PER JOURNAL	595 gms.	595 gms.	595 gms.	638 gms.	689 gms.	689 gms.	689 gms.	689 gms.	
CONNECTING ROD	E3606	E3606	E3606	E3606	E3606T	E3606T	E3606T	E3606T	
CAMSHAFT ~ INLET	E3134 (EC 53)	E3134	E3134	E3134	E4819 (to 34 KC 55)	E4819	E4819	E4819	
~ EXHAUST	E3325 (EC 48 EC 27)	E3325	E3325	E3325	E4855 (EC 48 EC 27)	E4855	E4855	E4855	E
CAM FOLLOWERS (TAPPETS)	E3059	E3059	E3059	E3059	E3059	E3059	E3059	INT: E3059R EX: E6490	IN
CAM FOLLOWER RADIUS (INS)	³/₄	³/₄	³/₄	³/₄	³/₄	³/₄	³/₄	INT: 1¹/₈ IN EX:	IN
CAM FOLLOWER OIL FEED	DRAIN	DRAIN	DRAIN	DRAIN	DRAIN	DRAIN	DRAIN	PRESSURE	DR
OIL PUMP	E3072	E3072	E3072	E3072	E3878	E3878	E3878	E5878	E
FEED PLUNGER	GS153	GS153	GS153	GS153	GS153	GS153	GS153	GS153	
FEED PLUNGER DIAMETER (INS)	0.3744/7	0.3744/7	0.3744/7	0.3744/7	0.3744/7	0.3744/7	0.3744/7	0.3744/7	
SCAVENGE PLUNGER	E1476	E1476	E1476	E1476	E1476	E1476	E1476	E1476	
SCAVENGE PLUNGER DIAMETER (INS)	0.4369/72	0.4369/72	0.4369/72	0.4369/72	0.4369/72	0.4369/72	0.4369/72	0.4369/72	
OIL PRESSURE RELIEF VALVE	E2795	E2795	E4191	E4191	E4191	E4191	E5896	E5896	
CARBURETTERS ~ PART No	376/204	376/204	376/257	376/257	376/257	389/203(UK) 389/95-T120(C)	389/203(UK) 389/95-T120(C)	389/203-T120 389/95-T120(C)	38 38
FLOAT BOWL TYPE	14/611 REMOTE	14/624 REMOTE	MONOBLOC	MONOBLOC	MONOBLOC	MONOBLOC	MONOBLOC	MONOBLOC	
CHOKE SIZE	1¹⁄₁₆ IN.	1¹⁄₁₆ IN.	1¹⁄₁₆ IN.	1¹⁄₁₆ IN.	1¹⁄₁₆ IN.	1¹⁄₈ IN. 1³⁄₁₆ IN.-T120(W)	1¹⁄₈ IN. 1³⁄₁₆ IN.-T120(W)	1¹⁄₈ IN. 1³⁄₁₆ IN.-T120 T(W)	
MAIN JET	240	240	240	240	240	260 330-T120 (W)	260 330-T120 (W)	260 330-T120 T(W)	33
SLIDE / CUT-AWAY	376/3½	376/3½	376/3½	376/4	376/3½	389/3	389/3	389/4-T120 T(W)	
NEEDLE POSITION	C/3	C/3	C/3	C/3	C/2	D/3	D/3	D/2	
NEEDLE JET	0.1065	0.1065	0.1065	0.1065	0.1065	0.106	0.106	0.106	
PILOT	25	25	25	25	25	25	25	25	
CARBURETTER BALANCE PIPE	—	—	—	—	NIL	E4792	E4792	E4792	
AIR FILTER	NIL	NIL	NIL	NIL	NIL (EXTRA FA804)	NIL-T120 E5262-T120C(W)	NIL-T120 E5262-T120R,T120C	E5261-1ω-T120T(W) E6431-2ω-T120C(W)	

1968	1969	1970	1971	1972	1973	1974	1975	1976	1977	1978
DU 66246	DU 89904-6 / DU 90282 and JC 00101 onwards	JD 24849	HE 30001	HG 30870	JH 15366-T120 / JH 15435-T140	GJ 55101	DK 61000	HN 62501	GP 75000	HX 00100
71×82	71×82	71×82	71×82	71×82	75×82 To KH22018 / 76×82 from 18249	76×82	76×82	76×82	76×82	76×82
649	649	649	649	649	724 / 747	747	747	747	747	747
41@6.700 / 50@6.500	47@6.700 / 52@6.500	47@6.700 / 50@6.500	47@6.700 / 50@6.500		@7.000	@7000	@7000	@7000	@7000	@7000
E534B / E527 (T120)	E9418	E9418	E12356	E12807 / E13446	71-3023	71-3023	71-7007	71-7007	71-7007	71-7007
E5343 / R E5350 / E5350 / R E5562	E9550 / R E9551 / E9550 / R E9551	E9550 / R E9551 / E9550 / R E9551	E9550 / R E9551 / E9550 / R E9551	E12811 / E13302 / R E13302	71-3339 / R 71-3338 / 71-3339 / 8 71-3338	71-3339 / R 71-3338 / 71-3339 / R 71-3338	71-3339 / R 71-3338 / 71-3339 / R 71-3338	71-3339 / R 71-3338 / 71-3339 / R 71-3338	71-3339 / R 71-3338 / 71-3339 / R 71-3338	71-3339 / R 71-3338 / 71-3339 / R 71-3338
E9514	E9516	E9516	E9516	E9516	PUSH-IN	PUSH-IN	PUSH-IN	PUSH-IN	PUSH-IN	PUSH-IN
E4603 (1"19/32)	E4603 (1"19/32)	E4603 (1"19/32)	E4603 (1"19/32)	E4603 (1"19/32)	70-4603 (1"19/32)	70-4603 (1"19/32)	70-4603 (1"19/32)	70-4603 (1"19/32)	70-4603 (1"19/32)	70-4603 (1"19/32)
E2904 (1"7/16)	E2904 (1"7/16)	E2904 (1"7/16)	E2904 (1"7/16)	E2904 (1"7/16)	70-2904 (1"7/16)	70-2904 (1"7/16)	70-2904 (1"7/16)	70-2904 (1"7/16)	70-2904 (1"7/16)	70-2904 (1"7/16)
E3827	E3827	E3827	E3827	E3827 / 3294	71-3294	71-3294	71-3294	71-3294	71-3294	71-3294
E3828	E3828	E3828	E3828	E3828 / 3295	71-3295	71-3295	71-3295	71-3295	71-3295	71-3295
E4221 / E7400 (green spot)	E4221 / E7400	E4221 / E7400	E4221 / E7400	E4221 / E7400	70-4221 / 70-7400	70-4221 / 70-7400	70-4221 / 70-7400	70-4221 / 70-7400	70-4221 / 70-7400	70-4221 / 70-7400
E6439	E6439	E6439	E6439	E6439	71-3296	71-3296	71-3296	71-3296	71-3296	71-3296
E6304	E6304	E6304	E6304	E6304	75mm 71-3335 / 76mm 71-3679(EXP)	71-4055(UNF) / 71-4005	71-4005	71-4005	71-4005	71-4005
E6868 T120,T120R	E6868 T120,T120R	E9488	E9488	E9488	UK-71-3778 / USA-71-3676	UK-71-3778 / USA-71-3676	UK 71-3778 USA 71-3676	71-3778	71-3778	71-3778
E6868~9:1	E6868~9:1	9:1	9:1	9:1	UK-7.9:1 / USA-8.6:1	UK 7.9:1 USA 8.6:1	UK 7.9:1 USA 8.6:1	7.9:1	7.9:1	7.9:1
E2620	E2620	E2620	E2620	E2620	71-3330	71-7330	71-7330	71-7330	71-7330	71-7330
E6000	E9349	E9349	E12575	E12575	71-3329	71-3329	71-3329	71-3329	71-3329	71-3329
E4.14-6	—	—	E11707	E11707	71-1707	71-1707	71-1707	71-1707	71-1707	71-1707
E7330	E9748	E11266	E11266	E11266	71-3677	71-3677	71-7001	71-7001	71-7001	71-7001
E5871	E9749	E11267	E12274 / E13098	E13098	71-3678	71-3678	71-7002	71-7002	71-7002	71-7021
E2879	E2879	E2879	E2879	E2879	70-2879	70-2879	70-2879	70-2879	70-2879	70-2879
E1591	E1591	E1591	E1591 / E3835	E3835 / METRIC	60-4167	60-4167	60-4167	60-4167	60-4167	60-4167
E4562	E4562	E4562	E12719	E12719	71-3666	71-3666	71-3666	71-3666	71-3666	71-3666
3	3	3	3	3	3	3	3	3	3	3
E4564	E4564	E4564	E4564	E4564	70-4564	70-4564	70-4564	70-4564	70-4564	70-4564
E6159	E6159	E6159	E6159	E6159	70-6159	70-6159	70-6159	70-6159	70-6159	70-6159
E4643	E4643	E4643	E4643 / E13097	E13097	71-3298	71-3298	71-3298	71-3298	71-3298	71-3298
E7332	E9687	E9687	E12425	E12425	71-2425	71-2425	71-2425	71-2425	71-2425	71-2425
E6328	E3907	E3907	E12601	E12799	71-3552	71-3552	71-3552	71-3552	71-3552	71-3552
85%	85%	85%	85%	85%	74%	74%	74%	74%	74%	74%
689 gms	689 gms	689 gms	689 gms	629 gms	689 gms	689 gms	689 gms	689 gms	689 gms	689 gms
E3606?	E9525	E9525	E9525	E9525	71-3006	71-3006	71-3006	71-3006	71-3006	71-3006
E4819	E10040 10.34 ICSS	E11063 10.34 ICSS	E11063	E11063	71-3011	71-3011	70-7016	70-7016	70-7016	70-7016
E5047	E10041 20.55 EC.34	E9989	E9989	E9989	71-3010	71-3010	70-7017	70-7017	70-7017	70-7017
IN. E3059R / EX. E8801	IN. E3059R / EX. E8801	IN. E3059R / EX. E8801	IN. E3059R / EX. E8801	IN. E3059R / EX. E8801	IN. E3059R / EX. 70-8801	IN. 70-7008 / EX. 70-8801	IN. 71-7008 / EX. 70-8801	IN. 71-7008 / EX. 70-8801	IN. 71-7008 / EX. 70-8801	IN. 71-7008 / EX. 70-8801
1 1/8 IN.	1 1/8	1 1/8	1 1/8	1 1/8	IN. 3/4 / EX. 1 1/8	IN. 3/4 / EX. 1 1/8	IN. 3/4 / EX. 1 1/8	IN. 3/4 / EX. 1 1/8	IN. 3/4 / EX. 1 1/8	IN. 3/4 / EX. 1 1/8
TIMED PRESSURE	TIMED PRESSURE	TIMED PRESSURE	TIMED PRESSURE	TIMED PRESSURE	TIMED PRESSURE	TIMED PRESSURE	TIMED PRESSURE	TIMED PRESSURE	TIMED PRESSURE	TIMED PRESSURE
E6928 / E9421	E6928 E9421	E9421	E9421	E9421	70-9421	70-9421	70-9421	70-9421	70-9421	70-9421
GS 153	GS153 E9269	E9269	E9269	E9269	70-9269	70-9269	70-9269	70-9269	70-9269	70-9269
0.3744/7	03/44/7 0.40615	0.40615	0.40615	0.40615	0.40585 0.40615	0.40585 0.40615	0.40585 0.40615	0.40585 0.40615	0.40585 0.40615	0.40585 0.40615
E6681	E6681	E6681	E6681	E6681	70-6681	70-6681	70-6681	70-6681	70-6681	70-6681
0.4868/71	0.4868/71	0.4868/71	0.4868/71	0.4868/71	0.4868/71	0.4868/71	0.4868/71	0.4868/71	0.4868/71	0.4868/71
E5896	E6595	E6595	E12210	E6595	70-6595	71-3447	71-3447	71-3447	71-3447	71-3447
R.930/9 L.930/10	R.930/9 L.930/10	R.930/43 L.930/44	R.930/66 L.930/67	R.930/66 L.930/67	R.930/88 L.930/67	R.930/92 L.930/92	R.930/92 L.930/93	R.930/92 L.930/93	R.930/92 L.930/93	R.930/92 L.930/93
CONCENTRIC	CONCENTRIC	CONCENTRIC	CONCENTRIC	CONCENTRIC	CONCENTRIC	CONCENTRIC	CONCENTRIC	CONCENTRIC	CONCENTRIC	CONCENTRIC
30 M.M.	30 M.M.	30 M.M.	30 M.M.	30 M.M.	30 M.M.	30 M.M.	30 M.M.	30 M.M.	30 M.M.	30 M.M.
220	190 T120 / 220 T120R	-T120 -T120R	180	180 T120 / 190 T120R	210	210	210	190	190	190
928/660/3	928/660/3	928/660/3	928/660/3	928/660/3	928/660/3	928/660/3	928/660/3	928/660/3	928/660/3	928/660/3
STD/MIDDLE	STD/MIDDLE	STD/2	STD/1	STD/1	STD/1	STD/1	STD/1	STD/1	STD/1	STD/1
0.106	0.106	0.106	0.106	0.106	0.106	0.106	0.106	0.106	.106	
20	—	—	—	—	—	—	—	—	—	
E4792	E4792	E4792	E4792	E4792	71-3577	71-3577	71-3577	71-3577	71-3577	
F8196	F8196	F11536	D3618 / D3072	D3072	60-3618	60-3618	60-3618	80-4265	60-4265	60-4265

	1959	1960	1961	1962	1963	1964	1965	1966	19
PRIMARY TRANSMISSION									
ENGINE DRIVE SPROCKET	E3108/24	E3108/22	E3108/21	E3108/21	E4572-DUPLEX	E5446-UK&GEN E5450 (C)	E5446-T120,T120R E5450 US(W)-C	E6446 T120, T120R E5450 U.S.T.T.	E544 E546
Nº OF TEETH	24	22	21	21	29	29	29	29	
CLUTCH SPROCKET	T1549	T1549	T1549	T1549	T1570	T1570	T1570	T1570	T
Nº OF TEETH	43	43	43	43	58	58	58	58	
CLUTCH SHOCKABSORBER SPIDER	T1041	T1041	T1041	T1041	T1721	T1721	T1721	T1721	T
Nº OF VANES	4	4	4	4	3	3	3	3	
CLUTCH PLATE - PART Nº - DRIVE	T1362	T1362	T1362	T1362	T1362	UK - T1362 USA - T1865	T1362	T1362	T
DRIVEN	T1363	T1363	T1363	T1363	T1363	T1363	T1363	T1363	
CLUTCH PLATE - QTY. - DRIVE	5	5	5	5	6	6	6	6	
DRIVEN	6	6	6	6	6	6	6	6	
CLUTCH SPRING	T1560	T1560	T1560	T1560	T1769	T1830	T1830	T1830	T
PRIMARY CHAIN	½ IN. × 0.305 IN.	½ IN. × 0.305 IN.	½ IN. × 0.305 IN.	½ IN. × 0.305 IN.	⅜ IN. DUPLEX	⅜ IN. DUPLEX	⅜ IN. DUPLEX	⅜ IN. DUPLEX	⅜ IN
Nº OF LINKS	70	70	70	70	84	84	84	84	
PRIMARY CHAINCASE CAPACITY	¼ PT.-150cc	¼ PT.-150cc	¼ PT.-150cc	¼ PT.-150cc	⅝ PT.-350cc	⅝ PT.-350cc	⅝ PT.-350cc	⅝ PT.-350cc	⅝ P
GEARBOX									
GEARBOX ASSEMBLY - PART Nº	T1583 (SEPARATE)	T1583 (SEPARATE)	T1583 (SEPARATE)	T1583 (SEPARATE)	INTEGRAL	INTEGRAL	INTEGRAL	INTEGRAL	IN
MAINSHAFT PART Nº	T914 (16T)	T914 (16T)	T914 (16T)	T914 (16T)	T914 (16T)	T914 (16T)	T914 (16T)	T914 (16T)	T91
LAYSHAFT PART Nº	T1063 (20T)	T1063 (20T)	T1608 (20T)	T1608 (20T)	T1843 (20T)	T1843 (20T)	T1843 (20T)	T1843 (20T)	T184
LAYSHAFT BUSH/BEARING PART Nº	T1367	T1367	T1606/T1614	T1606/T1614	T1606/T1614	T1606/T1614	T1606/T1614	T1606/T1614	T160
OVERALL RATIO 1ST (TOP)	11·20	11·38	11·92	11·92	11·81	11·81	11·81	T1208 T120R 11·81 / T120TT 13·20	T120 11·8
2ND	7·75	7·88	8·25	8·25	8·17	8·17	8·17	8·17 / 9·15	8·1
3RD	5·45	5·55	5·81	5·81	5·76	5·76	5·76	5·76 / 6·45	5·7
4TH	4·57	4·66	4·88	4·88	4·88	4·88	4·88	4·81 / 8·41	4·
5TH	—	—	—	—	—	—	—	—	
GEARBOX CAMPLATE	T500	T500	T500	T500	T500	T500	T500	T500	
INDEX PLUNGER	T44	T44	T44	T44	T44	T44	T44	T44	
INDEX PLUNGER SPRING	T373	T1604	T1604	T1604	T373	T373	T373	T373	
GEARBOX DRIVE SPROCKET	T417A	T417A	T417A'	T417A	T1715	T1916-17T-US(W)-C T1918-19T-US(C) T1918-19T-UK&GE	T1916-17T-US(W)-C T1917-18T-US(C) T1918-19T-UK&GE	T1916-17T, T120T.T. T1918-19T, T120,T120R	T916-1 T918-1
Nº OF TEETH	18	18	18	18	19				
SPLINE	AS T1382	AS T1382	AS T1382	AS T1382	AS T1382	AS T1914	AS T1914	AS T1914	AS
GEARBOX CAPACITY	⅔ PT.-400cc	⅔ PT.-400cc	⅔ PT.-400cc	⅔ PT.-400cc	⅞ PT.-500cc	⅞ PT.-500cc	⅞ PT.-500cc	⅞ PT.-500cc	⅞
REAR CHAIN SIZE	⅝ × ⅜ IN.	⅝ × ⅜ IN.	⅝ × ⅜ IN.	⅝ × ⅜ IN.	⅝ × ⅜ IN.	⅝ × ⅜ IN.	⅝ × ⅜ IN.	⅝ × ⅜ IN.	⅝ ×
Nº OF LINKS	101	98	98	98	103	102 (W-C) 103 T120 & T120R	102 (W-C) 103 T120 & T120R	102 T120 T.T. 103 T120 & T120R	104
FOLDING KICKSTART	T1270	T1270	T1270	T1270	T1270	T1938	T1938	T2113	T
FRAME									
FRAME - FRONT	F4414 SINGLE TUBE	F4608 DUPLEX	F4846 DUPLEX	F4846 DUPLEX	F5448 SINGLE TUBE	F5448	F6442	F6903	F
HEAD ANGLE	64½°	67°	65°	65°	65°	65°	65°	62°	
FRAME - REAR	F3635	F4609	F4609	F4609	F5449	F5449	F6443	F6904	F
SWINGING ARM	F4131	F4131	F4131	F4131	F5302	F5302	F5302	F6933	
PETROL TANK - HOME & GEN. EXPORT - GAL IMP	4	4	4	4	4	4	4	4	
PART NUMBER	F4115	F4640	F4640	F4640	F5260	F5260	F5260	FT004 -T120	F7o
COLOUR	TANGERINE/ PEARL GREY ROYAL BLUE / PEARL GREY	PEARL GREY TOP AZURE BLUE LOWER	SKY BLUE TOP SILVER LOWER	SKY BLUE TOP SILVER LOWER	ALASKAN WHITE	GOLD TOP ALASKAN WHITE LOWER	PACIFIC BLUE TOP SILVER LOWER	GRENADIER RED TOP ALASKAN WHITE LOWER	ALASK GOL
U.S.A - GAL	3 (IMP)	3 (IMP)	3 (IMP)	3 (IMP)	3 (IMP)	3 (IMP)	3 (IMP)	2½ (U.S)	
PART NUMBER	F4116	F4700	F4700	F4700	F5416	F5416	F5416	F6728 - T120R&M	F6T2
COLOUR	TANGERINE/ PEARL GREY	PEARL GREY TOP AZURE BLUE LOWER	SKY BLUE TOP SILVER LOWER	FLAME TOP SILVER SHEEN LOWER	ALASKAN WHITE	GOLD TOP ALASKAN WHITE LOWER	PACIFIC BLUE TOP SILVER LOWER HALF	GRENADIER RED TOP ALASKAN WHITE LOWER	AU BLU GOL
PARCEL GRID	F3917	F3917	F3917	F3917	F3917	F3917	F3917	F3917	F
KNEE GRIP	F2551/2	F2551/2	F2551/2	F2551/2	F1605/6	F1605/6	F5401/2-4GAL F1605/6-3GAL	F5401/2	F
TANK BADGE - HOME & GEN. EXPORT	F4127/8	F4766/7	F4766/7	F4766/7	F4766/7	F4766/7 - 4GAL F4127/8 - 3GAL	F4766/7 - 4GAL F4127/8 - 3GAL	F6887/8	F6
- U.S.A.	F4127/8	F4127/8	F4127/8	F4127/8	F4127/8	F4127/8	F4127/8	F6887/8	F6
TANK FIXING BOLT/SECURING STRAP	4 × FIXING BOLTS	SECURING STRAP F4658 & F4689	SECURING STRAP F4893	SECURING STRAP F4819 - 4 GAL F4817 - 4 GAL	3 × FIXING BOLTS	3 × FIXING BOLTS	3 × FIXING BOLTS	3 × FIXING BOLTS	3 × FI
PETROL TAP - MAIN/RESERVE - PART Nº	F3057	F3057	F3057	F4971/2	F4971/2	F4971/2	F4971/2	F4971/2	
BATTERY BOX - PART Nº	F4528	F4706	F4706 F4906	F4905	SWITCH PANEL - F5394	F5394	F5394	F6931-T120,T120R F6942 - T120 T.T.	E
COLOUR	PEARL GREY	PEARL GREY	SILVER	BLACK - HOME SILVER - U.S.A	BLACK	BLACK	BLACK	BLACK	E
OIL TANK - PART Nº	F4529	F4702	F4702	F5066	F5327	F6038	F6038	F6877	F
COLOUR	PEARL GREY	PEARL GREY	SILVER	BLACK - HOME SILVER - U.S.A	BLACK	BLACK	BLACK	BLACK	E
CAPACITY - PINTS	5 IMP	5 IMP	5 IMP	5 IMP	5 IMP	5 IMP	5 IMP	5 IMP	

1968	1969	1970	1971	1972	1973	1974	1975	1976	1977	1978
E5446	E5446	E5450	E12662	E12662	71-3542	71-3542	71-3542	71-3542	71-3542	71-3542
29	29	29	29	29	29	29	29	29	29	29
T1570	T1570	T1570	T1570	T1570	57-4640	57-4640	57-4640	57-4640	57-4640	57-4640
58	58	58	58	58	58	58	58	58	58	58
T2538	T2538	T2538	T2538	T2538	57-4636	57-4636	57-4636	57-4636	57-4636	57-4636
3	3	3	3	3	3	3	3	3	3	3
T1362	T1362	T1362	T1362	T1362	57-1362	57-1362	57-1362	57-1362	57-1362	57-1362
T1363	T1363	T1363	T1363	T1363	57-1363	57-1363	57-1363	57-1363	57-1363	57-1363
6	6	6	6	6	6	6	6	6	6	6
6	6	6	6	6	6	6	6	6	6	6
T1830	T1830	T1830	T1830	T1830	57-4644	57-4644	57-4644	57-4644	57-4644	57-4644
3/8 in. Duplex	3/8 in. Duplex	3/8 in. Duplex	3/8 in. Duplex	3/8 in. Duplex	3/8 in. Triplex	3/8 in. Triplex	3/8 in. Triplex	3/8 in. Triplex	3/8 in. Triplex	3/8 in. Triplex
84	84	84	84	84	84	84	84	84	84	84
5/8 PT.-350cc	5/8 PT.-350cc	5/8 PT.-350cc	1/4 PT.-150cc INITIAL FILL ONLY	1/4 PT.-150cc INITIAL FILL ONLY	1/4 PT.-150cc INITIAL FILL ONLY	1/4 PT.-150cc INITIAL FILL ONLY	1/4 PT.-150cc INITIAL FILL ONLY	1/4 PT.-150cc INITIAL FILL ONLY	1/4 PT.-150cc INITIAL FILL ONLY	1/4 PT.-150cc INITIAL FILL ONLY
INTEGRAL	INTEGRAL	INTEGRAL	INTEGRAL	INTEGRAL	INTEGRAL	INTEGRAL	INTEGRAL	INTEGRAL	INTEGRAL	INTEGRAL
T2436(16T)	T3893 / T4158	T4158(16T)	T4158(16T)	T4158(16T) / T4432	57-4432	57-4432	57-4432	57-4432	57-4432	57-4432
T2093(20T)	T3864 / T4155	T4155(20T)	T4345(20T)	T4345(20T) / T4548	57-4548	57-4900	57-4900	57-4900	57-4900	57-4900
T1606/T1614	T1606/T1614	T1606/T1614	T1606/T1614	T1606/T1614	57-1606/57-1614	57-1606/57-1614	57-1606/57-1614	57-1606/57-1614	57-1606/57-1614	57-1606/57-1614
11·81	11·81	11·81	12·10	4 SPEED 12·10 / 5 SPEED 12·78	12·23	12·23	12·23	12·23	12·23	12·23
8·17	8·17	8·17	8·36	8·36 / 9·10	8·63	8·63	8·63	8·63	8·63	8·63
5·76	6·00	6·00	6·15	6·15 / 6·92	6·58	6·58	6·58	6·58	6·58	6·58
4·84	4·84	4·84	4·95	4·95 / 5·89	5·59	5·59	5·59	5·59	5·59	5·59
—	—	—	—	4·95	4·70	4·70	4·70	4·70	4·70	4·70
T3650	T3650 / T4055	T4055	T4055	T4055 / T4360	57-4624	57-4624	57-4624	57-4889	57-4889	57-4889
T44	T3660	T3660	LEAF SPRING	LEAF SPRING	57-3660	57-3660	57-3660	57-7020	57-7020	57-7020
T373	T3661	T3661 / T4288/9	T4288/9	T4288/9	57-4459	57-4459	57-4459	57-4459	57-4459	57-4459
T1918	T1918	T1918	T1918	T1918 / T4397	57-4533	57-4782	57-4782	57-4782	57-4782	57-4782
19	19	19	19	19 / 19	20	20	20	20	20	20
AS T2316	AS T3891	AS T4332	AS T4332	AS T4332 / AS T4536	AS 57-4628	AS 57-4779	AS 57-4779	AS 57-4779	AS 57-4779	AS 57-4779
7/8 PT.-500cc	7/8 PT.-500cc	7/8 PT.-500cc	7/8 PT.-500cc	7/8 PT.-500cc	7/8 PT.-500cc	7/8 PT.-500cc	7/8 PT.-500cc	7/8 PT.-500cc	7/8 PT.-500cc	7/8 PT.-500cc
5/8 × 3/8 IN	5/8 × 3/8 IN	5/8 × 3/8 IN	5/8 × 3/8 IN.	5/8 × 3/8 IN.	5/8 × 3/8 IN.	5/8 × 3/8 IN.	5/8 × 3/8 IN.	5/8 × 3/8 IN	5/8 × 3/8 IN.	5/8 × 3/8 IN.
104	104	104	106	106	107	107	107	107	107	107
T2113	T3632	T3632	T3632	T3632	57-3632	57-3632	57-3632	57-7018	57-7018	57-7018
F7843	F7843	F11354	F12089	F14283 / F14578	83-4753	83-4753	83-4753	83-7032	83-7032	83-7032
62°	62°	62°	62°	62°						
F8036	F8036	F8036	—	—	—	—	—	—	—	—
F7845	F10045	F10045	F12513	F12513	83-2513	83-2513	83-2513	83-7035	83-7035	83-7035
4	4	4	4	4	4	4	4	4	4	4
F7004-T120 Hi-Fi Scarlet Top Silver Lower	F9704-T120 Olympic Flame Top Silver Lower	F11800 Astral Red Silver Side Panels	F12881 Tiger Gold Black Side Panels	F12881 Tiger Gold White Side Panels	83-4891 Two-Hi-Fi Vermillion-Gold Scallops T120-Purple-Gold White	83-5418 Two-Cherokee Red Gold White Scallops T120-Purple-Gold White	83-5418 Two-Cherokee Red Cold White Scallops T120-Purple-Gold White	83-7062 Poly-Red / 83-7063 Poly-Blue	83-7062 Poly-Red / 83-7063 Poly-Blue	83-7115 Tawny Brown/Gold / 83-7116 Poly-Blue
2½(U.S.)	2½(U.S.)	2½(U.S.)	3(U.S.)	3(U.S.)	2½(U.S.)	3·6(U.S.)	3·6(U.S.)	3·6(U.S.)	3·6(U.S.)	3·6(U.S.)
F6T28-T120R Hi-Fi Scarlet Top Silver Lower	F92OT-T120R Olympic Flame Top Silver Lower	F11789 Astral Red Silver Side Panels	F12996 Tiger Gold Black Side Panels	F12996 Tiger Gold White Side Panels	83-4861 Two-Hi-Fi Vermillion T120-Purple-Gold White	83-5413 Two-Cherokee Red Cold White Scallops T120-Purple-Gold White	83-5413 Two-Cherokee Red Cold White Scallops T120-Purple-Gold White	83-5413 Poly-Red	83-5413 Poly-Red	83-7111 Tawny Brown/Gold 83-7112 Royal Blue/Silver Black/Chocolate Red 83-7101 Aquamarine
F3917	—	—	—	—	—	—	—	—	—	—
F8192/3	F8192/3	F8192/3	—	—	—	—	83-4355/6	83-4355/6	83-4355/6	83-4355/6
F6887/8	F9700/1-4GAL FII340/1-3GAL	F9700/1-4GAL FII340/1-3GAL	F9700/1	F9700/1	82-9700/1	82-9700/1	60-2569	60-2569	60-2569	60-2569
F6887/8	F11340/1	F11340/1	F9700/1	F9700/1	82-9700/1	82-9700/1	82-9700/1	82-9700/1	82-9700/1	82-9700/1
3x Fixing Bolts	3x Fixing Bolts	3x Fixing Bolts	1x Centre Fixing Bolt	1x Centre Fixing Bolt	1x Centre Fixing Bolt	1x Centre Fixing Bolt	1x Centre Fixing Bolt	1x Centre Fixing Bolt	1x Centre Fixing Bolt	1x Centre Fixing Bolt
F4971/2 Tool Box/Side F8042	F4971/2 F8042	F4971/2 F8042	F12800/1 F12502 side panel/F12751 side cover	F12800/1 F13905 panel/F13860 cover	83-2800/1 83-4854 panel/83-4809 cover	83-2800/1 83-4854 panel/83-4809 cover	83-2800/1 83-4854 panel/83-4809 cover	60-4511/2 83-7067 cover	60-4511/2 83-7067 cover	60-4511/2 Styling panels 83-7111-Black
BLACK	BLACK	BLACK	BLACK	BLACK	BLACK	BLACK	BLACK	BLACK	BLACK	83-7099-Tawny Brown 83-7101-Aquamarine
F7836	F7836	FII763 / F13290	F12502 side cover/F12751 side cover	F13905 panel/F13851 cover	83-4803 panel/83-4810 cover	83-4803 panel/83-4810 cover	83-4803 panel/83-4810 cover	83-4854 panel/83-7068 cover	83-4854 panel/83-7069 cover	Styling panels 83-7093-Black
BLACK	BLACK	BLACK	BLACK	BLACK	BLACK	BLACK	BLACK	BLACK	BLACK	83-7100-Tawny Brown 83-7102-Aquamarine
5 IMP	5 IMP	5½ IMP / 6 IMP	4·8 U.S	4·8 U.S	4·8 U.S	4·8 U.S	4·8 U.S.	4·8 U.S.	4·8 U.S.	4·8 U.S.

		1959	1960	1961	1962	1963	1964	1965	1966	19
FRONT FORKS										
FORK ASSEMBLY		H1198	H1131	H1131	H1131	H1532	H1715-UK & G.E. H1716-US.(E-C). H1717-US. (W-C).	H1924-T120, T120R H1925-T120 T.T.	H1924-T120, T120R H1925-T120 T.T.	H2111 - H2112 - H2113 -
TOP LUG		H663A	H1287	H1287	H1287	H1528A	H1528A	H1528A	H1528A-T120, T120R H1287-T120 T.T.	H21
CROWN & STEM		H1229	H1283	H1283	H1287	H1577	H1577	H1577	H1577-T120, T120R H1899-T120 T.T.	H2109 H2110
DAMPER ASSEMBLY		H1106	H1124	H1124	H1124	H1124	H1653 SLEEVE H1383 NUT H1499 RESTRICTOR	H1896 SLEEVE H1058 NUT H1499 RESTRICTOR } H1913 ASSY T120TT	H1896 SLEEVE H1058 NUT H1499 RESTRICTOR } H1913 ASSY T120TT	H1896 SLE H1058 N H1499 REST
FORK SPRING	– INTERNAL	H384	H1300	H1300	H1300	H1473	–	–	–	
	– EXTERNAL	–	–	–	–	–	H1660	H1891-T120, T120R H1892-T120 TT	H1891-T120-T120R H1892-T120TT	H1891- H1892
	– RATE (LB/IN.)					32	30	26½ 32½	26½ 32½	2 3
	– COLOUR IDENT	RED	BLACK/WHITE	BLACK/WHITE	BLACK/WHITE	BLACK/GREEN	UNPAINTED	YELLOW/BLUE YELLOW/GREEN	YELLOW/BLUE YELLOW/GREEN	YELLO YELLO
OIL GRADE. (S.A.E)		20	20W/30	20W/30	20W/30	20W/30	20W/30			
QUANTITY PER LEG.		1/6PT. (100cc)	1/4PT. (150cc)	1/4PT. (150cc)	1/4PT. (150cc)	1/4PT. (150cc)	1/3PT (190cc)	1/3PT. (190c.c.)	1/3PT. (190c.c.)	1/3PT. (
HANDLEBAR	– HOME & GEN. EXPORT	H1009	H811	H811	H811	H1484	H1484	H1871	H1871-T120 H1870-T120R	H187 H187
	– U.S.A	H1010	H1179	H1179	H1179	H1511	H1511	H1870	H1511-T120TT.	H151
FRONT WHEEL TYRE SIZE	– UK & G.E	3.25×19	3.25×19	3.25×19	3.25×19	3.25×18	3.25×18	3.25×18-T120	3.25×18-T120	3.00
	– U.S.A	3.25×19	3.25×19	3.25×19	3.25×19	3.25×18	3.25×19	3.25×19-T120R 3.50×19-T120T.T.	3.25×19-T120R 3.50×19-T120TT	3.25 3.50
FRONT BRAKE SHOE DIAMETER (INS.)		8 – W1337/8	8 – W1337/8	8 – W1410/11 → FULLY FLOATING	8 – W1410/11	8 – W1410/11	8 – W1410/11	8 – W1410/11	8 – W1732/3	8 – W
	– TYPE	F.W. HUB × 1 L.S.	F.W. HUB × 1 L.S.	F.W. HUB × 1 L.S.	F.W. HUB × 1 L.S.	F.W. HUB × 1 L.S.	F.W. HUB × 1 L.S.	F.W. HUB × 1 L.S.	F.W. HUB × 1 L.S.	F.W. H
FRONT MUDGUARD	– PART No	H1211 – HOME & GE H1255 – U.S.A	H1294 → SPORTS	H1294	H1294	H1478	H1675 – T120 H1677 – T120R & C(E) H1687 – T120C (W)	H1675 – T120 H1677 – T120R & C(E) H1687 – T120C (W)	H1675 – T120 H1997 – T120R H1687 – T120TT	H167 H199
	– MATERIAL	STEEL-PAINTED	STEEL-PAINTED	STEEL-PAINTED	STEEL-PAINTED	STEEL-PAINTED	STEEL-PAINTED (T120 T120R T120C(E)) ALLOY-T120C(W)	STEEL-PAINTED (T120 T120R T120C(E)) ALLOY-T120C(W)	STEEL-PAINTED -T120 STAINLESS-T120R ALLOY-T120TT	STEEL- STAINL
	– FINISH	PEARL GREY/TANGERINE STRIPE PEARL GREY ROYAL BLUE STRIPE	PEARL GREY BLUE STRIPE	SILVER SKY BLUE STRIPE	SILVER SKY BLUE STRIPE	ALASKAN WHITE GOLD STRIPE	ALASKAN WHITE GOLD STRIPE	SILVER PACIFIC BLUE STRIPE	ALASKAN WHITE GRENADIER RED STRIPE	AU GOLD
FRONT NUMBER PLATE.		F2698 CHROME BEADED	F2996 → SPORTS	F2996	F2996	F2996	F2996 U.K & G.E. F3363 T120R & C(E)	F5934 UK & GE F6435 T120R & C(E)	F6470	F6
SPEEDOMETER	– MPH	S467/107/L	SC5301/09	SC5301/26	SC5301/26	SC5301/23	SSM5001/00	SSM5001/00	SSM5001/00	SSM
	– KPH	S467/47/L	SC5301/18	SC5301/18	SC5301/18	SC5301/28	SSM5001/01	SSM5001/01	SSM5001/01	
TACHOMETER		NOT FITTED	NOT FITTED	NOT FITTED	NOT FITTED	RC1307/01	RSM3001/02	RSM3001/02	RSM3003/01	RSM
TACHOMETER DRIVE GEARBOX		–	–	–	–	CRANKCASE UNION ADAPTOR E4699	E4699	E5667	E5756	E
REAR WHEEL TYRE SIZE	– UK & G.E.	3.50×19	3.50×19	4.00×18	4.00×18	3.50×18	3.50×18	3.50×18	3.50×18	3.
	– U.S.A.	3.50×19	3.50×19	4.00×18	4.00×18	3.50×18	4.00×18	4.00×18	4.00×18	4.0
	– REAR BRAKE DIAM (INS.)	7	7	7	7	7	7	7	7	
	– SPROCKET – Q.D.	W1040	W1376	W1376	W1376	W1040	W1040	W1040	W1040	W
	– BOLT-ON	W951	W1276	W1276	W1276	W951	W951	W951	W1498 DRUM W1499 SPROCKET	W14 W149
	– No OF TEETH	46	43	• 43	43	46	46	46	46	
REAR MUDGUARD	– PART No	F4394 VALANCED ←	F4681 → SPORTS	F4687	F4687	F5579	F5984-T120 & R. F5955-T120C (W)	F5984-T120 & R. F5955-T120C (W)	F5984 – T120 F6967 – T120R F5955 – T120 T.T.	F59 F59 F73
	– MATERIAL	STEEL-PAINTED	STEEL-PAINTED	STEEL-PAINTED	STEEL-PAINTED	STEEL-PAINTED	STEEL-PAINTED POLISHED ALLOY	STEEL-PAINTED-T120 & R POLISHED ALLOY-T120C(W)	STEEL PAINTED -T120 STAINLESS -T120R POLISHED ALLOY -T120T.T	STEEL STAIN
	– FINISH	PEARL GREY/TANGERINE STRIPE PEARL GREY ROYAL BLUE STRIPE	PEARL GREY BLUE STRIPE	SILVER SKY-BLUE STRIPE	SILVER SKY BLUE STRIPE	ALASKAN WHITE GOLD STRIPE	ALASKAN WHITE GOLD STRIPE	SILVER PACIFIC BLUE STRIPE	ALASKAN WHITE GRENADIER RED STRIPE	AL GO
REAR SUSPENSION UNIT		64054164	64054164	64054164	64054506	64054506	64054506-T120 64054164-T120R & C	64054506-T120 64054164-T120R & C	64054506-T120 64054164-T120R & T.T.	6405 6405
	– STROKE (INS)	2.2	2.2	2.2	2.5	2.5	2.5 2.2	2.5 2.2	2.5 2.2	
	– SPRING No	9054/280	9054/280	9054/280	64543818	SA253/5	SA253/5	SA253/5	SA253/5-T120 9054/280-T120R & T.T.	SA25 9054
	– COLOUR IDENT	GREEN/GREEN	GREEN/GREEN	GREEN/GREEN	BLUE/YELLOW	BLUE/YELLOW	BLUE/YELLOW	BLUE/YELLOW	BLUE/YELLOW GREEN/GREEN	BLUE GRE
	– RATE (LBS/IN)	100	100	100	145	145	145	145	145 100	
TWINSEAT	– PART No	F3785 – T120 F3647-2 LEVEL-U.S(E) F3786-VARLOW-U.S(W)	F4691	F4691	F4691	F5366	F5366 -T120 F5366A-T120R & C	F5366 -T120 F5366A-T120R & C(E)	F5366-T120 F5366A-T120R & C(E)	F777 F74
	– FINISH	BLACK	BLACK	BLACK	GREY	GREY	GREY	GREY	GREY	GRE
EXHAUST PIPE L.H.		E3628	E4133	E4133-T120, T120R E4177-T120C	E4133-T120, T120R E4177-T120C	E4716	E4716-UK & G.E E4884-ALL U.S.A	E5957-T120, T120R E4884-T120C (E) E5959-T120C (W)	E5957 T120, T120R E5959 T120T.T.	E59 E59
EXHAUST PIPE RH.		E3632	E3632	E3632-T120, T120R E4197-T120C	E3632-T120, T120R E4197-T120C	E4718	E4718-UK & G.E E4886-ALL U.S.A	E5958-T120, T120R E4846-T120C (E) E5961-T120C (W)	E5958 T120, T120R E5961 T120T.T.	E59 E59
CONNECTING PIPE		–	–	–	• –	–	–	–	–	
SILENCER L.H		E3651	E4118	E4118-T120, T120R E4132-T120C	E4174	E4949	E4949-UK & G.E. E4132-T120C(E)	E4949 – T120 E5866 – T120R E4132 – T120C(E)	E4949 -T120 E5866-T120R	E49 E59
SILENCER R.H		E3652	E4119	E4119-T120, T120R E4176-T120C	E4175	E4949	E4949-U.K. & G.E. E4176-T120C(E)	E4949 – T120 E5866 – T120R E4176 – T120C(E)	E4949 - T120 E5866-T120R	E49 E59
SILENCER MUTE		–	E4107	E4107	E4107	–	–	–	–	
EXTENSION PIPE		–	–	–	–	–	E4183 L} E4184 R} T120C (W)	–	–	

1968	1969	1970	1971	1972	1973	1974	1975	1976	1977	1978
H2283 - T120 H2285 - T120R	H3656 - T120 H3658 - T120R	H3907 - T120 H3909 - T120R	H4080	H4080	97-4396	97-4396	97-4396	97-4616 UKB-GE 97-4396-US	97-4616-UKBGE 97-4396-US	97-4616UKBGE 97-4396-US
H2100	H3667	H3667	H4035	H4035	97-4397	97-4381	97-4381	97-4381	97-4381	97-4381
H2278 - T120 H2280 - T120R	H3659 - T120 H2288 - T120R	H3659 - T120 H2288 - T120R	H4082 (16unf)	H4315 (24unf)	97-4385	97-4385	97-4385	97-4385	97-4385	97-4385
H2092 shuttle valve H2091 H2090	H2092 shuttle valve H2091 H2090	H2092 shuttle valve H2091 H2090	H4200	H4325	97-4325	97-4325	97-4325	97-4325	97-4325	97-4325
—	—	—	H4087	H4087	97-4011	97-4011	97-4011	97-4011	97-4011	97-4011
H1891-T120,T120R	H1891-T120,T120R	H1891-T120,T120R	—	—	—	—	—	—	—	—
26½	26½	26½	25	25	25	25	25	25	25	25
YELLOW/BLUE	YELLOW/BLUE	YELLOW/BLUE	ORANGE	ORANGE	ORANGE	ORANGE	ORANGE	ORANGE	ORANGE	ORANGE
⅓PT. (190cc)	⅓PT. (190cc)	⅓PT.(190cc)	⅓PT (190cc)	⅓PT.(190cc)	⅓PT.(190cc)	⅓PT.(190cc)	⅓PT.(190cc)	⅓PT.(190cc)	⅓PT.(190cc)	⅓PT.(190cc)
H1871-T120	H1871-T120	H1871-T120	H4252	H4252	97-4300	97-4300	97-7002	97-7002	97-7002	97-7002
H1870-T120R	H1870-T120R	H1870-T120R	H4252	H4252	97-4411	97-4411	97-7001	97-7001	97-7001	97-7001
3·00x19-T120	3·00x19-T120	3·00x19-T120	3·25x19-T120	3·25x19-T120	3·25x19	3·25x19	3·25x19	3·25x19	3·25x19	3·25x19
3·25x19-T120R	3·25x19-T120R	3·25x19-T120R	3·25x19-T120R	3·25x19-T120R	3·25x19	3·25x19	3·25x19	3·25x19	3·25x19	3·25x19
8-W1996	8-W1996	8-W1996	8-W3713	8-W3713	10-DISC	10-DISC	10-DISC	10-DISC	10-DISC	10-DISC
F.W.HUB x 2LS.	F.W.HUB x 2LS.	F.W.HUB x 2LS.	ALLOY HUB x 2LS.	ALLOY HUB x 2LS.	ALLOY HUB	ALLOY HUB	ALLOY HUB	ALLOY HUB	ALLOY HUB	ALLOY HUB
H2268-T120 H2276-T120R	H3882	H3882	H4268-T120 H4269-T120R	H4270-T120 H4271-T120R	97-4440-H&GE 97-4439-U.S.A	97-4440-H&GE 97-4439-U.S.A	97-4440-H&GE 97-4439-USA	97-7003	97-7003	97-7012/3/4/5 97-1013
STEEL-PAINTED T120 STAINLESS-T120R	STEEL PAINTED	STEEL PAINTED	STEEL PAINTED	STEEL-PAINTED	STEEL	STEEL	STEEL	STEEL	STEEL	STEEL
SILVER W.M SCARLET STRIPE	SILVER OLYMPIC FLAME STRIPE	ASTRAL RED SILVER STRIPE	TIGER GOLD BLACK STRIPE	TIGER GOLD GOLD WHITE STRIPE	CHROMED	CHROMED	CHROMED	CHROMED	CHROMED	PRINTED-HOME CHROMED-EXPORT
F6470	F10216 U.S.A N/A	F10216	F12834 + BLK PLASTIC	F12834	83-4823	83-4823	83-4823	—	—	—
SSM 5001/06	SSM 5001/06	SSM 5001/06	SSM 5007/00	SSM 5007/00	SSM 5007/00	SSM 5007/00	SSM 5007/00	SSM 4003/00	SSM 4003/00	SSM 4003/00
RSM 3003/01	RSM 3003/01	RSM 3003/01	RSM 3003/13	RSM 3003/13	RSM 3003/13	RSM 3003/13	RSM 3003/13	RSM 3006/00	RSM 3006/00	RSM 3006/00
E5756	E9331	E9331	E9331	E9331	71-2475	71-2475	71-2475	71-7011	71-7011	71-7011
3·50x18	3·50x18	3·50x18	4·00x18	4·00x18	4·00x18	4·00x18	4·00x18	4·00x18	4·00x18	4·00x18
4·00x18	4·00x18	4·00x18	4·00x18	4·00x18	4·00x18	4·00x18	4·00x18	4·00x18	4·00x18	4·00x18
7	7	7	7	7	7	7	7	10 IN. DISC	10 IN. DISC	10 IN. DISC
W1040	W1040	W1040	—	—	—	—	—	—	—	—
W1498 DRUM W1499 SPROCKET	W1498 DRUM W1499 SPROCKET	W3885 DRUM W1499 SPROCKET	W3747	W3747	37-3747	37-3747	—	37-7016	37-7016	37-7016
46	46	46	47	47	47	47	47	47	47	47
F8126-T120 F8144-T120R	F8126-T120 F8144-T120R	F11617-T120 F11619-T120R	F13566	F13566 F14595	83-4805	83-4805	83-4805	83-7031	83-7031	83-7123/4/5/6 83-7131
PAINTED STEEL STAINLESS-T120R	STEEL-PAINTED	STEEL-PAINTED	STEEL-PAINTED	STEEL-PAINTED	STEEL	STEEL	STEEL	STEEL	STEEL	STEEL
SILVER W.FI SCARLET STRIPE	SILVER OLYMPIC FLAME STRIPE	ASTRAL RED SILVER STRIPE	TIGER GOLD BLACK STRIPE	TIGER GOLD GOLD WHITE STRIPE	CHROMED	CHROMED	CHROMED	CHROMED	CHROMED	PRINTED-HOME CHROMED-EXPORT
64054806-T120 64054864-T120R	64062606-T120 64062607-T120R	64052806-T120 64052607-T120R	64062341	64052341 64052564	64052564	64052564	64052564	64052564	64052564	64052564-U.K. 1005600T-U.S.A.
2·5 2·2	2·5 2·2	2·5 2·2	2·2	2·2 2·0	2·0	2·0	2·0	2·0	2·0	2·0
SR253/5-T120 90SR/280T120R	64544234-T120 64543708-T120R	64544234-T120 64543708-T120R	64544754	64544754 64643708	64543708	64543708	64543708	64543708	64543708	64543708
BLUE/YELLOW GREEN/GREEN					GREEN/GREEN	GREEN/GREEN	GREEN/GREEN	GREEN/GREEN	GREEN/GREEN	GREEN/GREEN
145 100	145 CHROMED	145 100	110	110 100	100	100	100	100	100	100
F8205-T120 F8204-T120R	F9417	F11573	F13634	F14288 F14599	83-4786	83-4786	83-4786	83-7065	83-7065	83-7127-U.S. 83-7127-U.K (BLACK) 83-7129-U.K 83-7130-U.K
GREY (QUILTED)	GREY (QUILTED)	GREY (QUILTED)	GREY (QUILTED)	BLACK (QUILTED)	BLACK (QUILTED)	BLACK (QUILTED)	BLACK (QUILTED)	BLACK (QUILTED)	BLACK (QUILTED)	JUBILEE POWDER BLUE
E5957	E9363-T120 E9723-T120R	E9363	E12573	E12573 E12636	71-3755	71-3755	71-3755	71-3755	71-3755	71-3755
E5958	E9364-T120 E9723-T120R	E9364	E12573	E12576 E12637	71-3758	71-3758	71-3758	71-3758	71-3758	71-3758
—	E9368 E9888	E9888	E9888	E9888	70-9888	70-9888	70-9888	70-9888	70-9888	70-9888
E4949-T120 E5866-T120R	E5866	E5866	E11710-T120 E12382-T120R	E11710-T120/T140 E12382-T120R/T140	71-3723-T120 71-2382-T140	71-3999	71-3999	71-4159	71-4159	71-4159
E4949-T120 E5866-T120R	E5866	E5866	E11710-T120 E12382-T120R	E11710-T120/T140 E12382-T120R/T140	71-3723-T120 71-2382-T140	71-3999	71-3999	71-4159	71-4159	71-4159
—	—	—	—	—	—	—	—	—	—	—

163

	1959	1960	1961	1962	1963	1964	1965	1966	1967
MAGNETO — TYPE	K2F-42298(MANUAL)HLN K2FC-42364(AUTO) B.S.A.	K2F-42344(AUTO) B.S.C.6 K2FC-42364(AUTO) B.S.A.	K2F-42344(AUTO) B.S.C.6 K2FC-42364(AUTO) B.S.A. /USA	K2F-42344(AUTO) B.S.C.6 K2FC-42364(AUTO) B.S.A. /USA	CONTACT BREAKER ASSY.	47605 (4CA)	47605 (4CA)	47605 (4CA)	C.B. PLATE ASSY. 425879
CONTACT BREAKER — PART Nº	—	—	—	—	47605(4CA)	47602(4CA)-IG	47602(4CA)-COIL	47602(4CA)-T.T.	(4CA) 425879
— AUTO ADVANCE UNIT — PART Nº	—	47502	47502	47502	5441S750	COIL: 5441S750 E.T: 5441S746	COIL: 5441S750 E.T: 5441S746	COIL: 5441S750 E.T: 5441S746	COIL: 5441S750 E.T: 5441S746
— RANGE (º ENGINE)	30º	30º	30º	30º	28º	24º 10º	24º 10º	24º 10º	24º 10º
— STATIC TIMING (INS./ º BTC)	—	—	—	—	1/32 IN — 11º	1/16 IN — 15º 1/4 IN — 29º	1/16 IN — 15º 1/4 IN — 29º	1/16 IN — 15º 1/4 IN — 29º	1/16 IN — 15º 1/4 IN — 29º
— IGNITION FULLY ADVANCED (INS BTC)	7/16 IN	7/16 IN	7/16 IN	7/16 IN	0.435IN-39º	0.435IN-39º	0.435IN-39º	0.435IN-39º	0.435IN-39º
— POINTS GAP INS. MM	0.012 0.305	0.012 0.305	0.012 0.305	0.012 0.305	0.014-0.016 0.35-0.40	0.014-0.016 0.35-0.40	0.014-0.016 0.35-0.40	0.014-0.016 0.35-0.40	0.014-0.01 0.35-0.4
DYNAMO — LUCAS TYPE	E3L-L10-20035A	—	—	—	—	47164-T120 47188-T120C(U)	47162 47188-T120R	47162	47162
A.C. GENERATOR — STATOR	—	47134	47178	47162 47183 — U.S.A.	47162	47188-T120C(U)	47188-T120R 54213901	47188-T120TT 54213901	47188-T120TT 54213901
— ROTOR	—	423506	423506	5421390l (B/19)	54213901	54213B24-T120C(U)	54213B24-T120C(U)	54213B24-T120TT	54213B24-T120TT
BATTERY — PART Nº	PU7E-9	PU7E-9	PU7E-9	PU7E-9	MLZ-9E	MLZ-9E	MLZ-9E	PUZ-5A (PU22994→)	PUZ-5A
— VOLTAGE	6	6	6	6	6	6	6	12	12
HEADLAMP — TYPE	NACELLE	CHROMED Q.D. H/LAMP	CHROMED Q.D. H/LAMP	CHROMED Q.D. H/LAMP	CHROMED H/LAMP	CHROMED H/LAMP	CHROMED H/LAMP	CHROMED H/LAMP	CHROMED H/L
— LUCAS PART Nº	51860A	58556	58556	58878 58934	58934	58934	58934	59579	59579
— LIGHT UNIT Nº	55309	51679B	51679B	51679B	51679B	51679B	51679B	516812	516812
— BULB PART Nº	373(6V)L.H. DIP	312(6V) VERT. DIP	312(6V) VERT. DIP	312(6V) VERT. DIP	312(6V) VERT. DIP	312(6V) VERT. DIP	312(6V) VERT. DIP	414(12V) VERT. DIP	414(12V) VE DIP
— MAIN — WATTS	30	30	30	30	30	30	30	50	50
— DIP — WATTS	24	24	24	24	24	24	24	40	40
PILOT BULB — PART Nº	988	988	988	988	988	988	988	989	989
— WATTS	3 (M.C.C)	3 (M.C.C)	3 (M.C.C)	3 (M.C.C)	3 (M.C.C)	3 (M.C.C)	3 (M.C.C)	6 (M.C.C)	6 (M.C.C
IGNITION SWITCH	—	—	—	—	34427 (BBSA)	34427 (BBSA)	34427 (BBSA)	31899 (S.45)	31899 (S.
— LOCATION	SEE CUT-OUT	SEE CUT-OUT	SEE CUT-OUT	SEE CUT-OUT	L.H. SIDE PANEL BELOW SEAT YALE KEY (BTM)	L.H. SIDE PANEL BELOW SEAT YALE KEY (BTM)	L.H. SIDE PANEL BELOW SEAT YALE KEY (BTM)	BELOW SEAT L.H. SIDE PANEL YALE KEY (BTM)	BELOW SEAT L.H. SIDE PANEL YALE KEY (B
LIGHTING SWITCH	31371B	37B4 (41SA)	31784 (41SA)	37B4(41SA)	34289 (BBSA)	34289 (BBSA)	34289 (BBSA)	34289 (BBSA)	34289 (B
— LOCATION	NACELLE	BELOW SEAT, R.H.SIDE #46/7 BRACKETS	BELOW SEAT R.H. SIDE #46/7 BRACKETS	BELOW SEAT R.H.SIDE #5020/1 BRACKETS	BELOW SEAT, L.H. SIDE PANEL (TOP)	BELOW SEAT, L.H. SIDE PANEL (TOP)	BELOW SEAT L.H. SIDE PANEL (TOP)	BELOW SEAT L.H. SIDE PANEL (TOP)	HEADLAMP SH (BOTTOM)
COMBINED DIP SWITCH & HORN PUSH	31563A	31563	31563	31563	31563	31563	31563	31563	3156
H/BAR SWITCH ASSY L.H.	—	—	—	—	—	—	—	—	—
H/BAR SWITCH ASSY R.H.	—	—	—	—	—	—	—	—	—
CUT-OUT BUTTON	31011B-NACELLE	76200A-H/BAR	76200A-H/BAR	76200A-H/BAR	NONE	31516(55S)-T120C(w)	31576(55S)-T120C(w)	31566(55S)-T120R 31071(55S)-T120TT	31566(55S)-T
DIP SWITCH	—	—	—	—	—	—	—	—	—
HORN PUSH	—	—	—	—	—	—	—	D553-T120TT	D553-T12
AMMETER	36129A	3608A	3608A	36296 (2AR)	36296 (2AR)	36296 (2AR)	36296 (2AR)	36296 (2AR)	36296 (2AR
RECTIFIER	—	47132	47132	49072 (SILICON DIB447)	49072 (20S506)	49072 (20S506)	49072 (20S 506)	49072 (20S 506)	49072 (20S 5
ZENER DIODE	—	—	—	—	—	—	—	49345 (PLATE SINK)	49345 (BL
HORN	7004BA (HF1441)	7004BA (HF1441)	7004BA (HF1441)	70163 (8H)	70163 (8H)	70163 (8H)	70163 (8H)	70164 (8H)	70197 (6
STOP-TAIL LAMP	53432 (L564)	53432 (L564)	53432 (L564)	53432 (L564)	53432 (L564)	53432 (L564)	53432 (L564)-T120 53972(L679)-T120R	53454(L564)-T120 53473(L679)-T120R	53454(L564 53973(L679)
— BULB — WATTS-OFFSET PIN	384 - 6/18	384 - 6/18	384 - 6/18	384 - 6/18	384 - 6/18	384 - 6/18	384 - 6/18	380 - 6/21	380 - 6
STOP LAMP SWITCH	31383 (22B)	34279 (6SA)	34181 (LUCAR)	34181 (LUCAR)	31383 (22B)	31437 (22B)	31437 (22B)	31437 (22B)	31437 (22
IGNITION WARNING LIGHT — BULB	—	—	—	—	—	—	—	38189 BA7S GREEN 281 (2W)	38189 BA GREEN 281
— LOCATION	—	—	—	—	—	—	—	HEADLAMP SHELL	HEADLAMP S
MAIN BEAM WARNING LIGHT — BULB	—	—	—	—	—	—	•	38189 BA7S RED 281(2W)	38189 BA RED 281
— LOCATION	—	—	—	—	—	—	—	HEADLAMP SHELL	HEADLAMP
DIRECTION INDICATOR FLASHER LAMP	—	—	—	—	—	—	—	—	—
— BULB	—	—	—	—	—	—	—	—	—
FLASHER UNIT	—	—	—	—	—	—	—	—	—
FLASHER WARNING LIGHT-H/L SHELL	—	—	—	—	—	—	—	—	—
IGNITION COIL	—	—	—	—	45152 (MA6)	45152 (MA6) 45149 (3ET)	45152 (MA6) 45159 (3ET)	45151(MA6)-121-T120 45159(3ET) T120-TT N4	45147(MA N4 45159(3E
SPARK PLUG	N3, FE100, HLN	N3, FE100, HLN	N3, FE100, HLN	N4, FE100, HLN	N4, FE100, HLN	N5BR-T120C(U)	N5BR-T120C(U)	N5BR-T120C(U)	N5BR-T120C(U
SPARK PLUG GAP	0.020IN (0.50MM)	0.020IN (0.50MM)	0.020IN (0.50MM)	0.020IN (0.50MM)	0.020IN (0.50MM)	0.020IN (0.50MM)	0.020IN (0.50MM)	0.020IN (0.50MM)	0.020IN (0
FUSE RATING (AMPS)					25	25	25	35	35

1968	1969	1970	1971	1972	1973	1974	1975	1976	1977	1978
(6CA) 54419097	(6CA) 54419097	(6CA) 54419097	(6CA) 54419097	(6CA) 54419097	(10CA) 54425160	(10CA) 54425160	(10CA) 54425160	(10CA) 54425160	(10CA) 54425160	(10CA) 54425160
54419340	54419340	54419340	54419340	54419340	54425657	54425657	54425657	54425657	54425657	54425657
24°	24°	24°	24°	24°	24°	24°	24°	24°	24°	24°
1/16in -15°	1/16in -15°	1/16in -14°	0·60in 1·5mm -14°	0·60in 1·5mm -14°	0·60in 1·5mm -14°	0·60in 1·5mm -14°	0·60in 1·5mm -14°	0·60in 1·5mm -14°	0·60in 1·5mm -14°	0·60in 1·5mm -14°
0·435in -39°	0·435in -39°	0·415in -38° 0·4mm	0·415in -38°	0·415in -38°	0·415in -38° 10·4mm	0·415in -38° 10·4mm	0·415in -38° 10·4mm	0·415in -38° 10·4mm	0·415in -38° 10·4mm	0·415in -38° 10·4mm
0·014-0·016 0·35-0·40	0·014-0·016 0·35-0·40	0·014-0·016 0·35-0·40	0·014-0·016 0·35-0·40	0·014-0·016 0·35-0·40	0·014-0·016 0·35-0·40	0·014-0·016 0·35-0·40	0·014-0·016 0·35-0·40	0·014-0·016 0·35-0·40	0·014-0·016 0·35-0·40	0·014-0·016 0·35-0·40
—	—	—	—	—	—	—	—	—	—	—
47162	47205	47205	47205	47205	47205	47205	47205	47205	47205	47205
54213901	54213901	54213901	54213901	54213901	54213901	54213901	54213901	54213901	54213901	54213901
PUZ-5A	PUZ-5A	PUZ-5A	PUZ-5A	PUZ-5A	PUZ-5A	PUZ-5A	PUZ-5A	PUZ-5A	PUZ-5A	12N9-4B-1
12	12	12	12	12	12	12	12	12	12	12
CHROMED H/LAMP	CHROMED H/LAMP	CHROMED H/LAMP	CHROMED H/LAMP (FLAT PAN)	CHROMED H/LAMP (FLAT PAN)	CHROMED H/LAMP	CHROMED H/LAMP	CHROMED H/LAMP	CHROMED H/LAMP	CHROMED H/LAMP	CHROMED H/LAMP
59883	59883	59969	60262	60262	60512	60512	60512	60512	60512	60512
516798	516798	516798	54525272	54525272	516801	516801	516801	54525927	54525927	54511815
446 (12V) VERT. DIP	446 (12V) DIP	446 (12V) VERT. DIP	370 (12V) DIP	370 (12V) VERT. DIP	370 (12V) VERT. DIP	370 (12V) VERT. DIP	370 (12V) VERT. DIP	370 (12V) VERT. DIP	370 (12V) VERT. DIP	410 (12V) HALOGEN VERT. DIP
50	50	50	45	45	45	45	45	45	45	45
40	40	40	35	35	35	35	35	35	35	40
989	989	989	989	989	989	989	989	989	989	989
6 (M.C.C)	6 (M.C.C)	6 (M.C.C)	6 (M.C.C)	6 (M.C.C)	6 (M.C.C)	6 (M.C.C)	6 (M.C.C)	6 (M.C.C)	6 (M.C.C)	6 (M.C.C)
31899 (S45)	31899 (S45)	31899 (S45)	39565 (1493A)	39565 (1495A)	31899 (S45)	31899 (S45)	31899 (S45)	54531899 (S45)	54531899 (S45)	54531899 (S45)
L.H. FORK TOP COVER	L.H. FORK TOP COVER	L.H. FORK TOP COVER	R.H. PANEL BELOW SEAT	R.H. PANEL BELOW SEAT	L.H. FORK COVER	L.H. FORK COVER	L.H. FORK COVER	L.H. FORK COVER	L.H. FORK COVER	L.H. FORK COVER
35710 (S75A)	35710 (S75A)	35710 (S75A)	31276	31276	34419 (S75A)	34419 (S75A)	34419 (S75A)	34419 (S75A)	34419 (3/4)	34419 (S75A)
HEADLAMP SHELL (TOGGLE)	HEADLAMP SHELL (TOGGLE)	HEADLAMP SHELL (TOGGLE)	HEADLAMP SHELL 2 POSITION-ROTARY	HEADLAMP SHELL 2 POSITION-ROTARY	HEADLAMP SHELL (TOGGLE)	HEADLAMP SHELL (TOGGLE)	HEADLAMP SHELL (TOGGLE)	HEADLAMP SHELL (TOGGLE)	HEADLAMP SHELL (TOGGLE)	HEADLAMP SHELL (TOGGLE)
31563	31563	31563	39595	39595	39595	39595	39595	30447	30447	30447
—	—	—	39596	39596	54033751	54033751	54033751	30781	30781	30781
NOT FITTED	NOT FITTED	NOT FITTED	SWITCH CONSOLE RT. H/BAR	SWITCH CONSOLE L.H. H/BAR	SWITCH CONSOLE L.H. H/BAR	SWITCH CONSOLE L.H. H/BAR	SWITCH CONSOLE L.H. H/BAR	SWITCH CONSOLE RT. H/BAR	SWITCH CONSOLE RT. H/BAR	SWITCH CONSOLE RT. H/BAR
—	—	—	SWITCH CONSOLE L.H. H/BAR	SWITCH CONSOLE RT. H/BAR	SWITCH CONSOLE RT. H/BAR	SWITCH CONSOLE RT. H/BAR	SWITCH CONSOLE RT. H/BAR	SWITCH CONSOLE L.H. H/BAR	SWITCH CONSOLE L.H. H/BAR	SWITCH CONSOLE L.H. H/BAR
—	—	—	SWITCH CONSOLE L.H. H/BAR	SWITCH CONSOLE RT. H/BAR	SWITCH CONSOLE RT. H/BAR	SWITCH CONSOLE RT. H/BAR	SWITCH CONSOLE RT. H/BAR	SWITCH CONSOLE RT. H/BAR	SWITCH CONSOLE L.H. H/BAR	SWITCH CONSOLE L.H. H/BAR
36403 (2AR)	36403 (2AR)	36403 (2AR)	—	—	—	—	—	—	—	—
49072 (2DS 506)	49072 (2DS 506)	49072 (2DS 506)	49072 (2DS 506)	49072 (2DS 506)	49072 (2DS 506)	49072 (2DS 306)	49072 (2DS 506)	49072 (2DS 506)	49072 (2DS 506)	49072 (2DS 506)
49345 (FINNED) SINK	49345 (FINNED) SINK	49345 (FINNED) SINK	49345 INSTRUMENT MOUNTING PLATFORM	49345 INSIDE AIR F.	49345 INSIDE AIR FILTER	49345 INSIDE AIR FILTER	49345 INSIDE AIR FILTER	49345 INSIDE AIR FILTER	49345 INSIDE AIR FILTER	49345 INSIDE AIR FILTER
70197 (6H)	01900 (LARGE) DT101 (SMALL)	D2256 (SMALL) DT257 (LARGE)	70216 (6H)	70228 (6H)	70228 (6H)	70228 (6H)	70228 (6H)	70228 (6H)	70228 (6H)	70228 (6H)
53454 (L564) -T120 53973 (L679) -T120R	53454 (L564) -T120 53973 (L679) -T120R	53454 (L564) -T120 53973 (L679) -T120R	53973 (L679)	53973 (L679)	56513 (L917)	56513 (L917)	56513 (L917)	56515 (L917)	56515 (L917)	56515 (L917)
380 - 6/21	380 - 6/21	380 - 6/21	380 - 6/21	380 - 6/21	380 - 6/21	380 - 6/21	380 - 6/21	380 - 6/21	380 - 6/21	380 - 6/21
31437 (22B)	F: D2085 R:54033764 (22B)	F: D2085 R: 31437 (22B)	F: N/A R: 34815 (118SA)	34815 (118SA)	34815 (118SA)	34815 (118SA)	34815 (118SA)	34815 (118SA)	34815 (118SA)	34815 (118SA)
38189 GREEN BATS 281 (2W)	38189 RED BATS 281 (2W)	38189 RED BATS 281 (2W)	54363464 RED BATS 281 (2W)	54363454 RED BATS 281 (2W)	54363454 RED BATS 281 (2W)	54363454 RED BATS 281 (2W)	54363454 RED BATS 281 (2W)	54363454 RED BATS 281 (2W)	54363454 RED BATS 281 (2W)	54363454 RED BATS 281 (2W)
38189 RED BATS	38189 BATS RED	38189 BATS GREEN	54363455 BATS	54363455 BATS	54363455 GREEN BATS 281 (2W)	54363455 GREEN BATS 281 (2W)	54363455 GREEN BATS 281 (2W)	54363455 GREEN BATS 281 (2W)	54363455 GREEN BATS 281 (2W)	54363455 GREEN BATS 281 (2W)
HEADLAMP SHELL	—	—	HEADLAMP SHELL	HEADLAMP SHELL	HEADLAMP SHELL	HEADLAMP SHELL	HEADLAMP SHELL	HEADLAMP SHELL	HEADLAMP SHELL	HEADLAMP SHELL
—	—	—	56147	56147	56147	56147	56147	56559	56559	56559
—	—	—	382 (21 WATT)	382 (21 WATT)	382 (21 WATT)	382 (21 WATT)	382 (21 WATT)	382 (21 WATT)	382 (21 WATT)	382 (21 WATT)
—	—	—	35048	35048	35048	35048	35048	35048	35048	35048
45110 (MA12) -T120 46300 (MA12) -T120R H/BAR	45110 (MA12)	45223 (17M12)	45223 (17M12)	54363453 AMBER BATS 281 (2W)	54363453 AMBER BATS 281 (2W)	54363453 AMBER BATS 281 (2W)	54363453 AMBER BATS 281 (2W)	54363453 AMBER BATS 281 (2W)	54363453 AMBER BATS 281 (2W)	54363453 AMBER BATS 281 (2W)
				45223 (17M12)	45223 (17M12)	45223 (17M12)	45223 (17M12)	45223 (17M12)	45223 (17M12)	45223 (17M12)
N3	N3	N3	N3	N3	N3	N3	N3	N3	N3	N3
0·25in (0·635mm)	0·25in (0·635mm)	0·25in (0·635mm)	0·25in (0·635mm)	0·25in (0·635mm)	0·25in (0·635mm)	0·25in (0·635mm)	0·25in (0·635mm)	0·25in (0·635mm)	0·25in (0·635mm)	0·25in (0·635mm)
35	35	35	35	35	35	35	35	35	35	35